OUT OF EDEN

Jay Jardine

THE CHOIR PRESS

First published in the United Kingdom in 2017 by
The Choir Press

ISBN 978-1-911589-28-0

ACKNOWLEDGEMENTS

I am deeply grateful to my husband Douglas, who, from the first time we met, was fascinated by my heritage. It was he who encouraged me to convert a tentative concept into something our family, and especially our granddaughters, could cherish forever. Whenever I expressed doubts about finishing my book, he heartened and inspired me to achieve my goal.

I am also greatly indebted to my brother Patrick, who assisted me immensely in describing what life was like on Eden Estate.

Thanks also to Jill, Cecelia and Jeannie, my cousins in Australia, for their contributions of photographs – especially Jeannie Stanley, whose information from our family tree was invaluable.

My Uncle Jim in Plymouth should also be thanked for his patience and for providing me with factual material which assisted me greatly.

CHAPTER 1

Hapur, India, 1938

Kathleen was sitting on the veranda reading one of her favourite classics. Her coffee-coloured skin was a perfect mix of her mother and father. It was a hot afternoon and the fans on the veranda were working hard. She looked up from her book and smiled as she admired her beautiful surroundings. She was twelve years old and had just come home from nine months at boarding school in Mussoorie in the foothills of the Himalayas and was looking forward to the three-month break on her beloved Eden.

Eden Estate was situated about 10 miles outside Hapur, in the state of Uttar Pradesh, which borders Nepal and seven other Indian states including the National Capital Territory of Delhi.

It was a magnificent property set in 120 acres of land. The family were the major produce growers for the region, growing mangos, cotton, sugar cane, guava, peaches and melons. Life was good, although it hadn't always been so, prior to her mother's marriage to Nester Freese.

Sometimes she had to pinch herself to make sure it wasn't all a dream – Eden Estate was truly beautiful and she knew she was privileged. She never forgot how life could have been for the family following the death of her father. She was twelve when the accident happened and the memory of that day would haunt her forever.

Nester Freese had inherited Eden Estate from his parents, Edward James Freese and his wife Edith. Edith had won the Epsom Derby and with the proceeds they built Eden Estate, which Edward designed single-handedly. Together they had seven children, all of whom died young except Nester and his sister Albine. Nester's first wife Rose Agnes O'Grady tragically died giving birth to their daughter Marie.

Edward James Freese

Edward's wife Edith Beard

Rose Agnes O'Grady – Nester's first wife, who died giving birth to
Marie, Kathleen's step-sister

CHAPTER 2

Kathleen looked forward to going on their small boat with her father and her siblings when she came home for the holidays. Her father, Henry Charles Stanley, was English and, at over six feet tall with blue-grey eyes and dark hair, he was a very striking figure. Kathleen sat with her father at the back of the boat while her two younger siblings took up their usual positions – Joyce at the front and James in the middle. The two younger ones were dangling their home-made fishing rods over the side of the boat. They had fashioned their rods from small bamboo canes, using a length of string on which they'd attached a hook. They looked forward to going fishing with their father and the fact they never caught so much as a minnow pleased Kathleen immensely, as she couldn't bear to see the poor things being hooked by their mouths; worse still was the thought of removing the hook from the mouth of the fish.

Henry had taught Kathleen how to steer the boat and she was eager to take the rudder whenever he went for a swim. He was an extremely powerful swimmer and had represented his high school when he was a teenager and never lost his love of the sport. He never swam far from the boat for any length of time to ensure he'd be able to make it back quickly if required, all the time checking on the children repeatedly.

They were trying a different stretch of water that day, a little further down than the usual run. Her father was reluctant to let her take the rudder in waters they were not familiar with, but Kathleen was keen to show him she was capable and could navigate as usual. A little way down the river her father decided to go in for a swim and handed the rudder over to Kathleen. After he dived in, she looked behind her to check on her siblings, who were happily fishing as usual, but when she turned and faced downriver, she couldn't see her father. She didn't want to alarm Joyce and James and thought he'd briefly gone underwater, but after what seemed like an eternity, he didn't come up. She started to call him, and the children started to panic. She scanned the surface of the water frantically, at the same time shouting to Joyce to take the rudder while she looked for the rope, but Joyce just stood there staring into the water while James cried hysterically. They were no use at all.

She remembered the dreadful swimming lessons at school and wished now more than ever that she had learned to swim, but she had a mortal fear of water. It always struck her father as strange, that someone who was afraid of water enjoyed going out on the boat. She wished she could dive in and save her father but all she could do was to watch in horror as he was carried further and further downriver towards the rapids.

She saw her father's hand reach out from the water. She let go of the rudder, grabbed the rope and threw it to him, but the rope slipped through his fingers and he was dragged downstream, heading towards the rapids. As the boat neared the rapids Kathleen knew she had a choice to make, either to go after him or turn back and get her siblings to safety. She grabbed the rudder and turned the boat around. Her siblings were hysterical by now but all she could think of was getting them to safety.

The inquest revealed that particular stretch of water concealed strong undercurrents and even though there was nothing she could have done, Kathleen always blamed herself for not being able to swim. No words of consolation from her mother would ease the guilt she felt, not even when Birdi pointed out how brave she was in saving her siblings.

CHAPTER 3

———⚬⊙⊙⚬———

At the time of her father's death, Kathleen's mother Birdith (affectionately known as Birdi) was Matron at Dumbarnie Boarding School in Mussourie and it was there she met Marie Freese, a five-year-old girl who was her daughter Naomi's best friend. The girls introduced their parents to each other and later that year their parents married. Nester brought Birdi and her seven children to live at Eden Estate.

The road to the main house on Eden was lined with peach trees and the fragrance from the peaches on approaching the property was exceptionally breath-taking. The house was built of red brick, in a quadrant style with three sections for the family while the other section housed the servants' quarters. The adjacent building was used as a store room for sugar-cakes, attar flour, rice and lentils for the family's personal use.

Birdi, Eric and James at the back of the house

Nester Freese

Birdith Brenda Stanley

Top row: James, Eric, Marie, Eric's wife and Malcom
Sitting: Nester, Birdi and friends

Eric on horseback with James standing behind

Out of Eden

One of the more formal lounges was situated on the relatively cooler west wing, which housed a library of books. This was Kathleen's favourite room of all: not only was it cooler, but her siblings, who didn't share her love of reading, hardly ever went in there. She could often be found on the sofa, sound asleep with the open book face downwards on her chest. The right-hand side of the room housed a large library with a sliding ladder attached to a rail for access to the books on the higher shelves. Four large ceiling fans with rattan sails ran constantly to keep the room cool.

Friday was the night the family got together for dinner. The table could seat twenty-four and every Friday Kathleen's aunts, uncles and cousins would gather for a special dinner. Anjana, the head cook, and her staff always made something special for the Friday get-together, which was eagerly anticipated by the family.

After dinner, which would often take at least three hours, the children would go off and amuse themselves elsewhere – the older ones would congregate in the library to play records on the gramophone. The grown-ups would sit for hours and talk about the day's events on the plantation for the first part of the evening, then usually Birdi would bring out the cards and gin rummy would go on late into the night.

Kathleen listening to music

Kathleen aged 16 in the peach groves

The day lounge had been designed in a palm court style, the beautiful rattan and wooden furniture, high-backed peacock chairs and sumptuous soft furnishings all in typical colonial style. The floor had a large Indian rug and a beautiful hand-carved coffee table where Birdi ate breakfast. The two large parlour palms on each side of the French doors produced a dappled effect on the marble floor when the sun shone through their spindly leaves. The French doors leading out to the garden were opened early in the morning, revealing the magnificent manicured gardens. This was Birdi's favourite room. She wakened everyday around 5:30 and enjoyed this quiet time to herself and, as she sipped her tea, she would use this time to plan the day ahead before the rest of the house stirred.

Soon the servants would be preparing breakfast for the rest of the family. The silence would be broken by Anjana, barking orders to her two assistants. She wasn't as bad as she made herself out to be and beneath her hard exterior she was a kind woman. Birdi knew Anjana was giving the leftover food to her family, who lived in a nearby village. For years she'd seen a boy crossing the garden late at night with the food from the kitchen wrapped in a gunny sack, the same type of sack used to store the sugar-cakes held in the food store and although Birdi knew, she never said anything to Anjana. Birdi often reflected upon the fact that it could so easily have been one of her sons taking hand-outs.

The fully equipped kitchen was Anjana's pride and joy. The entire length of the back wall housed a two-tiered shelving unit for copper pots, fish kettles, rice pans and every kind of modern gadget available. To the left of the shelves stood two large tandoor ovens, one for home-made breads like chapattis, parathas and flatbreads, the other for meat and fowl. The other side of the kitchen had a similar housing unit, where the crockery was kept all neatly stacked according to plate size.

Anjana and her staff were getting everything ready for breakfast when she heard the sounds of falling pots and pans resonate through the kitchen. She turned to see Joyce's pet monkey running amok along the shelves, knocking everything down in its path. This wasn't the first time the monkey had devastated the kitchen. Anjana chased the monkey with a broom but this only made the animal more edgy and caused further damage. It wasn't the first time, she complained to Birdi and declared she wasn't cooking anymore until the monkey was tied up outside. Joyce pleaded with her mother not to have the monkey kept outside but Anjana got her wish.

The monkey was relegated to new quarters – James built a six-foot wooden tower with a feeding platform on the top, where it spent most of the time eating and sleeping.

Nester, Birdi and the two older boys, James and Eric, ran Eden Estate. Eric and his family occupied the west wing of the property and James and Marie occupied a separate home on Eden.

James had completely renovated and extended two of the older buildings on the estate, which he'd made into one large house. James' wife Marie had a real talent when it came to gardening and designed the gardens from scratch. There was a wooden pavilion at the back of the house which provided much-needed shade from the afternoon sun and was where Marie spent hours tending to her favourite orchids and Hindu rope plants, which snaked down the posts of the pavilion. Taller plants and trees such as banana, bamboo and bottle gourds had been planted around the perimeter. Marie was also an accomplished cook and occasionally liked to use the bottle gourds in her curries, which, she maintained, gave the curry a nutty flavour.

Malcolm, Birdi's third son, was in his second year at the University of Delhi in New Delhi. Like Kathleen, Malcolm appreciated books and even as a young boy he never showed an interest in the business – his dreams lay elsewhere.

James and Marie on their wedding day

CHAPTER 4

One day, Eric was underneath one of the tractors, which had the two front wheels propped up on blocks. He was trying to replace a rusted ball joint which was refusing to co-operate. Frustrated by the lack of progress, he hammered the knuckle with such force that the blocks supporting the wheels collapsed, pinning his legs under the tractor.

James and Majeet were on the other side of the yard putting Mya back into her compound after returning from a neighbouring farm. Nester had found the elephant wandering about on the land after she'd been orphaned as a baby. When she was old enough to be trained, Majeet was employed as her handler and occasionally Mya was loaned out to neighbouring smallholdings when they needed help. The work wasn't hard and she never worked more than a couple of hours – it was more fun for her than work.

She appeared to look forward to the days she went out because as soon as she saw Majeet walking towards the compound she would toss her head up and down and trumpet loudly and, in any case, Mya didn't do anything she didn't want to. She could be stubborn at times.

As they were closing the gates to Mya's compound, they heard Eric cry out in pain and came running to help. They tried to lift the front of the tractor but it was too heavy so they ran back and got Mya out. Majeet got her to lift the axle with her trunk, and they pulled Eric out from under the tractor, but it was obvious his right leg was badly broken. The accident had brought it home to him that he'd be no good to his family if he were incapacitated for any length of time and besides, there was always the chance it may happen again and someone else might not be so lucky. The old tractor was banished to the barn and a brand new John Deer tractor replaced it.

While this was going on, the monkey had been screeching loudly but nobody took any notice, thinking it was harassed by Mya being so close.

When they turned to see what was distressing the monkey, they saw a rabid dog making its way towards the house – probably looking for food – and it was heading towards the monkey's food, which had fallen from the feeding platform at the top of the pole. The monkey was on the ground and as the dog approached it tried to escape to safety, back up to the feeding platform, but the dog pounced on it and bit the monkey on its hind quarters. Within a few hours it became evident the poor animal had contracted rabies and James had to shoot it. The next day James took his shotgun and went looking for the dog. He found it hiding in one of the outbuildings and as he moved closer towards it, he could see the dog foaming at the mouth. He took aim and shot it.

James on the new tractor

CHAPTER 5

Birdi's birthday was coming up and a lavish party was being planned. Invitations had been sent out to all their friends, including Doug and his wife Jean. Doug was a Regimental Sergeant Major in the Royal Artillery and was stationed in Peshawar. Birdi and Jean had become great friends and often met for lunch when Birdi went to the market in her horse and trap to buy Anjana's spices. She was a familiar figure to the traders and vendors, not least because she was one of the major employers in the region, but also it was unusual to see a woman driving herself. They would make way for the horse and trap when she came to the market with some even calling her 'memsab', which she didn't much care for as she didn't consider herself to be any better than others.

It was on one of these trips to the market when she saw a little boy lying at the side of the road; his bicycle with both wheels buckled was lying beside him.

She stopped the horse, went over to help him and when she turned him over she recognised him. He was about seven years old. She'd seen him many times at the market buying two sacks of attar and loading them onto his bicycle. His face was bleeding and when she tried to lift him he winced with pain – his right arm was broken. She put him in the back of the trap and the boy directed her to his home.

The house was in a very poor part of Hapur with families crowded into small one-roomed houses in narrow back-streets and no sanitation. Birdi couldn't leave the horse and trap at the top of the narrow street as it probably wouldn't be there when she got back. Consequently, with great difficulty, she slowly manoeuvred the trap to the boy's house, taking care not to damage what little possessions these people had in the form of pots, grinding stones and tandoors outside their doors.

Birdi helped the boy get down from the trap just as his mother was coming out of the house. When she saw his face covered in blood she assumed Birdi was responsible and began shouting and crying. The boy explained to her that this woman was only trying to help and told his mother it was a rickshaw that had knocked him off his bicycle. Life in India was cheap if you were poor and another child being injured or killed by a rickshaw didn't warrant a driver to stop.

At the hospital, as they were waiting for Arjun's arm to be re-set, his mother Panjiri told Birdi how difficult it would be without Arjun being able to go to the market or do his chores. Panjiri's husband had been killed in the rioting in the Punjab and they had fled to Hapur with nothing but the clothes they stood in. They were both painfully thin and malnourished and Birdi knew she had to help them.

She visited Arjun and his mother a few days later and realised just how much Panjiri relied on her son's help, so she offered to take them to Eden until his arm had mended. At first Panjiri was determined not to take charity but Birdi convinced her it would only be until Arjun could work again. Birdi was constantly helping people. She deliberated the plight of Panjiri and her son with Nester and he agreed it would be in their best interests to come and live at Eden. When they got to Eden, Birdi introduced them to the servants and told them that Panjiri and her son would be staying for a while with them. Arjun soon became a favourite at Eden. He was a sweet, gentle boy with big, brown, heavily lashed eyes. Arjun means 'bright' or 'shining' in Hindu and Panjiri had given him the name because of his beautiful eyes.

As the weeks passed, Birdi noticed that Panjiri had started to help the other women around the house and Arjun seemed much happier now his cast was off. He loved going to see Mya. Majeet allowed him to feed her and he'd watch intently when Majeet tended to her feet. But his favourite thing, by far, was when Eric let him sit on the tractor because 'he was going to be a farmer one day'.

Birdi knew there was no future for either of them if they returned to their village and she couldn't help but notice that Nester had grown fond of Arjun – perhaps he felt he was the son he would never have, following Rose's premature death. Birdi asked Panjiri if she would like to stay on and work at Eden and Arjun could go to school. The enormous smile on Panjiri's face and the tears running down her cheeks was all the answer Birdi needed.

Birdi never forgot she'd been given a second chance and had used it to build a new life for her family – now she had the ability to change Panjiri and Arjun's lives forever.

CHAPTER 6

When Jean got her invitation to the party, she phoned Birdi to ask if she could bring her nephew with them. Preparations were underway for the party. The peach trees which lined the road to the house were linked by lights to the main building, as were the trees directly outside Birdi's favourite room. The French doors were open and the scent of the flowers in the evening breeze was magnificent.

Anjana and her staff had been working hard for days preparing the food. Extra tables had been set up in the large dining hall and were laden with delicacies of all kind.

Birdi was a Seven Day Adventist and although she never touched alcohol she didn't judge people who did. A bar had been set up at the other end of the hall and waiters employed for the evening.

She'd intended to employ caterers to give Anjana and her staff a night off, but Anjana had insisted she wanted to make the food, adding that it wouldn't be as good as hers anyway, so Birdi conceded and let her have her wish.

First to arrive were the Americans from the base. They were always first for any party at Eden. They brought the latest American records from the States and lots of Glen Miller music, which Birdi adored. The girls looked forward to the Americans coming over as the boys would teach them the latest dance from the States. Even Kathleen had learned to Jive a little although she wouldn't be allowed to stay up late at the party until she was sixteen. At ten o'clock the girls would be sent upstairs but they'd sneak back out and peer through the spindles on the bannister to watch the fun.

Some of the officers had private accommodation in the city and Birdi was friendly with their wives. The girls looked forward to seeing the American wives in the latest fashions from the States and it was evident, when the girls were older, that their dress sense had been influenced by the American women.

The party was in full swing and the girls were upstairs peering through the bannister as usual. Uncle Doug and Aunt Jean came in accompanied by a handsome young soldier. As soon as she saw him, Kathleen knew he was the one. She once had a dream and in it she'd seen a white man with blue-grey eyes. He was dressed in khaki but she couldn't see his face clearly because of the smoke and the heat shimmer from the burning scrub the field hands were tending to. She only saw him fleetingly in her dream but she knew it was him.

Bill in 'khaki'

It was time for the girls to go back to boarding school until next summer. There was a break of one week at Christmas. Kathleen was a brilliant student and gained a certificate with Honours in Religious Knowledge and was now studying for her Senior Cambridge qualifications to become a teacher.

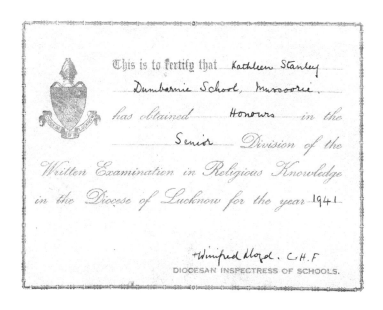

This is to certify that Kathleen Stanley Dumbarnie School, Mussoorie, has obtained Honours in the Senior Division of the Written Examination in Religious Knowledge in the Diocese of Lucknow for the year 1941

+Winifred Lloyd. C.H.F
DIOCESAN INSPECTRESS OF SCHOOLS.

Kathleen at boarding school in Mussoorie Second row,
right-hand side

CHAPTER 7

Kathleen was looking forward to coming home for Christmas. She was hoping the handsome young soldier would be at the Christmas party. It was a much smaller affair than the usual parties at Eden, just for family and close friends.

The girls arrived from boarding school as preparations were being made for Christmas. James was in the process of grappling with the ten-foot tree, trying to position it in the stand he'd made and the girls were growing impatient, waiting to dress it. Anjana and her staff were busy in the kitchen and the wonderful aroma of food being cooked was permeating into the hall making the girls' mouths water.

On Christmas Day the family were opening their presents which had been lovingly wrapped by Birdi. She'd always favoured the American way of doing this – each parcel wrapped in simple white crêpe paper tied with red satin ribbon. She was watching the children opening their presents and shrieking with delight but she couldn't help but notice that Kathleen seemed quiet and preoccupied. At first she thought she may be unwell since she hadn't even touched the sweet treats Anjana always brought out on Christmas morning, but Kathleen assured her mother she was fine and she'd probably have some later. Kathleen knew she wouldn't be able to eat much. Her stomach was full of butterflies at the thought of seeing Bill, who was coming for Christmas dinner with his aunt and uncle.

Bill hadn't met her yet. The first time he was at a party on Eden Estate, she'd been upstairs, peering through the bannister at him. It would be different today. Today they'd all be sitting round the table and she hoped she would be placed next to him. Her wish came true.

Birdi put the young ones at the bottom of the table. Kathleen, Joyce, James and Bill were sitting together. She hardly ate a thing, despite the fact that a few days earlier all she was looking forward to was gorging on the fabulous food Anjana produced.

Joyce engaged Bill in conversation but Kathleen couldn't bring herself to say anything; she was so nervous just sitting opposite him. Bill turned to her and asked about her love of hockey. He'd seen some pictures of the girls at boarding school dotted around the room and in one of them her team were standing behind a trophy which they had won. She was now in familiar territory and absorbed in conversation and soon found herself relaxing in his company. As she looked into his blue-grey eyes, which were almost the same colour as her father's had been, she was reassured that this was indeed the man of her dreams.

At the end of the meal, the four of them went outside to take in the evening air. They sat on the high-backed peacock chairs on the veranda, where they stayed until it was time for Bill to go. The said their goodbyes but Kathleen couldn't stop thinking about him and, as it happened, he of her. She couldn't wait until summer, when she would see him again. She wanted to know everything about him – where was he from, what were his parents like?

CHAPTER 8

―――∽⟨⟩∽―――

Bill was the oldest of eleven children and was born in Bandikui to domiciled European parents. There were over 1,000 British families living in Bandikui and, with the main Delhi Jaipur line halting there, it was the main source of employment.

Bill's father was employed by the railway and his job could sometimes take him away from home for several weeks at a time. He had a short temper which made the children nervous when they were around him and they looked forward to those days when he'd be working away. Bill's mother was a quiet, gentle woman whose family originated from Edinburgh, she who worked hard to keep her children fed and clothed, making most of the children's clothes by hand to make ends meet. Bill was the eldest and was especially close to his mother and although he'd never seen his father hit his mother, he was constantly protective of her.

It had been one of those days when his father had been in a foul mood. Bill had been beaten by his father and locked in the makeshift shed at the bottom of the garden without food or water. This was a regular punishment for the boys although lately Bill thought it was becoming a more frequent event, which he put down to the fact that his father had started gambling and money was as short as his temper. Bill always tried to protect his siblings and often took the beatings for them.

Whenever one of them was put in the shed, they would wait until their father was sleeping then take food and water to their unfortunate sibling. The 'hot-house', as it was known to the children, had a corrugated roof which reached extreme temperatures especially at midday, when the sun was at its height. The heat generated from the roof made it unbearable inside. As he endured his punishment, Bill was already making plans to get out of this life – he hated his father for his brutality. After three days, he was released from the hot-house and early the next day, before anyone was awake, he left home. He gathered a few belongings and some fruit, put them in a gunny sack and left his mother a note telling her he was going to enlist in the Army.

Bill's mother's sister, Jean, had married an Englishman who was a Regimental Sergeant Major in the Royal Artillery based in Lucknow. It was Bill's plan to find his uncle and, although he was only fifteen, he hoped his uncle would get him into the Army.

The journey from Bandikui to Lucknow was a little over 560 kilometres. Bill made his way across the country by riding trains, finding refuge in villages and towns and by doing odd jobs in return for food. He learned to cook like the Indians, taking his turn to gather the wood for the open fires on which they cooked their meals. The journey wasn't for the faint-hearted, especially at night, when bandits were out to take anything they could and he had a few narrow escapes.

One day he came across a building with a plaque on the wall which read 'The Christian Brotherhood'. He explained to them that he was trying to get to Lucknow to meet his uncle and asked if he could stay for a few days. He was delighted when they agreed. He was taken to a dormitory with about twenty beds and shown to his bed. The dormitory was empty as the other boys were all doing chores. The Brother told him to put his sack under the bed and to follow him downstairs, where he was put to work immediately.

They finished work at six and Bill followed the boys into the canteen. It was sparsely furnished with long tables and hard benches and as he joined the end of the queue one of the boys handed him a wooden bowl. As they filed along, one spoon of rice was put in the bowl and one spoon of dhal dolloped on top; the water was on the table. There was no talking at the table and when they finished their meal they were sent to the dorm and lights went out at 7:30 pm. Bill thought he could hear one of the boys crying but was too afraid to go to him in case he was caught out of bed. He covered his head with his pillow and tried to get some sleep. But sleep didn't come. He lay awake most of the night trying to work out what kind of place this was, then, just as he was dropping off, one of the Brothers unlocked the dorm at 5:30 am to get them up for work.

Breakfast was some kind of oats which looked like lumpy porridge and tasted awful, but he knew it would be all he would get until lunchtime so he forced it down. After breakfast the boys were given buckets and scrubbing brushes then allocated tasks which took them up to midday, at which time they were marched to the canteen for dhal, rice and water.

After lunch it was time for schooling, which, for the main part, was religious knowledge followed by handwriting classes as most of the boys couldn't write. Bill could read and write and enjoyed this latter part of the lesson. Not only was it a form of respite for him, it was also therapeutic. For a few brief hours, it allowed him to escape into another world where he didn't need to think how he was going to survive. He didn't realise he had an artistic talent until Brother Paul pointed out to him how good he was. He told Bill that he was different from the other boys and that he'd teach him the art of calligraphy, so Bill stayed an extra half hour each day after class for tuition.

Although life was hard, he wasn't being beaten on a regular basis the way he was at home, and in a strange way, because of the writing classes, he began to settle in and decided to stay a bit longer before resuming his journey to Lucknow. That was a decision he came to regret.

One night, Brother Paul woke Bill from his sleep and told him he had found a book with beautiful illustrations he might like. Bill followed the Brother down the corridor to his room; when Brother Paul opened the door, Bill saw the book lying on the bed.

Brother Paul sat down on the bed, looked at Bill and patted the bed, gesturing to him to sit beside him. It was indeed a beautiful book. Bill was engrossed in the fabulous images when suddenly the Brother pushed him down on the bed and sexually assaulted him. When his ordeal was over Bill ran to the door but it was locked. As the Brother started towards him, Bill grabbed the wooden stool beside the bed and swung it with force at the Brother's head. He saw him fall to the floor with blood oozing from his head. He looked for the key and found it in the pocket of the Brother's habit. He unlocked the door, ran downstairs through the kitchen and jumped out of an open window.

The next day he resumed his journey riding trains and living with the Indians as he crossed the country. However traumatic the journey, even being stolen from and beaten up by bandits, it was unquestionably preferable to staying with the Christian Brotherhood.

CHAPTER 9

❧❦❧

Bill only had the clothes he stood up in and after a few days on the dusty roads it became clear he would have to find some kind of work to replace the clothes he had to leave behind. He'd been following the course of the river wherever possible to avoid getting lost and came upon a fishing village. Men were bringing in their catches and he observed that as the boats were docking it was the job of one boy to jump into the water to tie them off.

Bill waited until the catch had been distributed between the fishermen and then approached one of the men, who appeared to be in charge. The man's dialect was different from that in Bandikui but he was able to understand most of what he said and vice versa. He told Bill that the boys who tied the boats off were the sons of the fishermen and therefore received no payment. The men only received payment once they'd sold their fish at the market.

As Bill walked away despondently, the man called him back and asked him why he was looking for work. Bill told him where he had come from and why he was trying to get to Lucknow. The fisherman looked at Bill's dishevelled, dirty clothing and told him to go and wash in the river then come back and he would take him to his home for some food.

When they entered the house Bill saw three little children sitting on the bare floor, watching their mother cooking. She was sitting cross-legged in front of a fire-pit, on which was balanced a wide, shallow pan. The aromatic blend of spices together with the colour was amazing. Sameer asked if he liked fish moulee and Bill replied he'd never tasted it before. Sameer's wife passed Bill a bowl which contained plain white rice with a ladle of fish moulee on top. He was already salivating at the sight and smell of the food and when he tasted it he wasn't disappointed. The mix of spices, coconut milk and turmeric was delectable.

After supper he went outside and lay on the riverbank against a small upturned boat. He hadn't felt this safe or satiated in a long time and with his stomach full, he drifted off to sleep.

Exhaustion and hunger had prevailed because when he woke he realised that the men had already gone out fishing.

He saw Sameer's wife and some of the other women of the village washing clothes at the side of the riverbank. She gestured to him to take his shirt off so she could wash it for him but he insisted he would do it himself. As he was washing his shirt, he could hear the women around him giggling – they'd obviously never seen a man washing clothes before.

Bill stayed with the family for a few weeks and in that time he learned how to cook and fish, skills he would find extremely useful on his journey.

On the day he left, Sameer and his wife gave him a cloth sack tied with a pull string, which contained attar flour, rice, a small flatplate and a billycan. There was also a clean shirt and a mundu – a kind of undyed cotton sarong which, when pulled up in the middle and tucked into the waistband, doubled as baggy shorts.

Sameer suggested it may be safer for Bill to adopt this attire while travelling and showed him how to tie a pagri – a type of turban. He also proposed Bill should blacken his face when approaching major towns and cities as a lone white traveller would prove easy prey for thieves and bandits. Bill took Sameer's advice and blackened up before leaving the village, but it had an adverse effect as it greatly enhanced his blue-grey eyes, making him even more distinctive. He would rely on the sun to colour his skin.

CHAPTER 10

⸺◦⟨∽⟩◦⸺

Sameer told Bill to make for Jhansi, which would bring him roughly halfway between Banduikui and Lucknow. From there he could ride a train to Lucknow, where his uncle was stationed.

He set off in the cool of the evening. He had been walking for three miles and it was beginning to get dark so he decided to make camp for the night. He gathered wood and built a fire and fetched some water from the river. He made chapattis from the attar, which he cooked on the flatplate, and boiled some rice in the billycan to accompany the fish he'd caught. On the days he didn't catch any fish, he spread some of Sameer's wife's home-made mango and lime pickle on the chapattis before filling them with rice. It wasn't the tastiest of meals but it dissipated the hunger pangs which otherwise would have kept him awake.

His time spent in the village and the kindness he'd been shown by Sameer and his wife had revitalised him. He felt stronger and more determined than ever to reach Lucknow and set off with a spring in his step. He hadn't been walking long when a farmer with a bullock cart loaded with melons stopped and asked him where he was going. He told Bill he could take him as far as his village. By the time they reached the village it was getting dark so he cooked his food and stayed overnight.

The next morning, he took stock of his supplies and realised that if he only travelled on foot for the rest of the journey, he would soon run out of food. The quickest way to reach Jhansi was by boat. There, the estuary he'd been following would merge with The Pahuj River and Jhansi was situated on the banks of the river. All that remained was to hitch a ride on one of the small boats carrying produce to the market.

When they reached Jhansi the first thing he saw was Jhansi Fort, a magnificent building situated on the top of the hill.

Bill helped Vishnu unload the goods from the boat onto his cousin's bullock cart and from there they took the produce to the market on Shivpuri Road, which was the biggest vegetable market in the area. When they reached the market they laid out the produce in crates and Bill helped to sell the vegetables. He didn't expect any payment because Vishnu had been kind in bringing him to Jhansi, but Vishnu gave Bill five rupees and thanked him for his help and directed him to the station. He made his way to Jhansi Junction and saw a goods train which was going to Lucknow and as it was pulling out he ran after it, jumped on and hid between the bales of grain and oilseeds.

When he reached Lucknow he found the barracks where his Uncle Doug was stationed and started a new life in the British Army.

CHAPTER 11

—◦⟨⊙⟩◦—

It was Kathleen's final year at boarding school, and she'd achieved the qualifications she needed to finish at the teacher training college. When she came home this time she wasn't planning on burying her head in her books. All she could think about was seeing Bill again.

A party had been arranged for her sixteenth birthday. The butterflies in her stomach wouldn't settle at the thought of seeing him again and her hands were shaking with excitement. She called Esther, her ayah, to help her dress. Her mother had chosen a pale blue dress for her which complimented her skin tone.

The Americans arrived first as usual and all the guys were astonished at the transformation of this little girl they knew as Katy, who used to peer down on them from the bannister. She was a woman in every sense of the word but tonight she only had eyes for one man. When she came downstairs she looked for him amongst the guests but he wasn't there. She joined her sisters, all the time watching the hallway.

Kathleen aged 16 wearing
her new dress her mother
bought her for the party

Bill at Eden on
leave

Bill on his wedding day

It wasn't long before Bill arrived with his aunt and uncle. She went to greet him and when they met, he could see what he was thinking. This young girl who had gone to school last year had come back a beautiful woman. Her exotic looks and coffee-coloured skin mesmerised him. He couldn't take his eyes off her. She was the most beautiful woman he'd ever seen.

Kathleen had to be seen to be spending time with her guests and family and continued to mingle until Birdi asked Anjana to bring out the birthday cake and as Kathleen cut it, she looked up at Bill with that special look only for him, who in turn was looking at her. Birdi had witnessed the exchange of looks between the two of them and when Kathleen asked if she and Bill could go outside for some fresh air, Birdi agreed on one condition: that her Nana chaperoned them. In the months that followed, they spent a lot of time together going for walks, sitting on the veranda and talking until late in the evening, all the time being chaperoned by Nana, who sometimes nodded off to the delight of Bill, when he'd seize the chance to steal a kiss.

Later that year they announced their engagement and were married on 2nd January 1943.

Top row left to right: James (brother), Joe Mulvaney (Bill's father), Eric (brother), Kathleen's mother Birdi, Barbara (Bill's sister), Joyce (Kathleen's sister), Ted (Bill's brother) and Kathleen's Nana.

Next row: Bridesmaids (Kathleen's friends from school), Marie, Malcolm (Kathleen's brother), Bill's mum with baby sister June.

Front row: Duncan and Rosemary (Bill's brother and sister), Bill, Kathleen, Barbara and Naomi.

CHAPTER 12

---❦---

Bill had been in with the Royal Artillery since 1938. It was now 1943 and he had just returned from Burma. While he was there he, like hundreds of others, contracted malaria. The soldiers had no resistance to malaria, rendering them unfit to fight. The disease had a major impact on the Army, often being responsible for more casualties than combat wounds and although it wasn't fatal it would take soldiers out of action for prolonged periods, which is exactly what happened to Bill. He, and others from the regiment, were sent back to Peshawar.

Burma played a significant part in World War II for the British Army and although the military had been trained in jungle warfare, the real problem was the environment: It proved extremely difficult to move heavy artillery through the mountain terrain.

The jungle was extremely impenetrable and remote to fight in, owing to the difficult terrain and climate making progress through the jungle frustratingly slow. The men had to cut through the jungle with machetes and normally only managed to cover little more than 500 yards a day. Moving casualties and wounded down the arduous terrain was equally as problematic.

The Japanese were a ferocious enemy and every soldier vowed to fight to the death for their country. Once they had joined the Imperial Army their lives were given over to Japan unequivocally.

Rangoon was extremely significant to the Japanese, which they perceived as a vital industrial supply line. Their aim was to prevent the Americans getting supplies to their long-term enemies, the Chinese, whom they had been fighting a war with since the early 1930s. Another reason was to obtain the industrial products for themselves, namely oil and rubber as they desperately needed resources to enable them to stay in the war. Burma was a strategic stronghold for the Japanese which they were not prepared to surrender and in June 1942 the Japanese were sitting right on the border of India – Britain's richest possession.

The Burma campaign lasted for four years before Britain finally regained control following Hiroshima and Nagasaki in 1945.

Bill (second from right)

Some of the men with the Gurkhas

Bill's regiment of the Royal Artillery

Some of the men with the company cook

Bill on right of picture

Ceremonial Guard of Honour (Bill on left)

CHAPTER 13

❦

In 1947, the Allied High Commission was re-shuffled and the Viceroy was replaced by the charismatic Lord Louis Mountbatten – the last Viceroy of India. Although he had little knowledge of Indian politics, he managed to persuade Gandhi and Nehru to agree to separation, but Jinnah, who represented the Indian Muslims, was hard to convince. However, once Mountbatten managed to get the leaders to agree, he changed the proposed date of transfer to 15th August, nine months earlier than had been agreed upon and many blamed him for the atrocities that followed. The speed with which the separation was carried out uprooted and displaced thousands of people. Armed groups, organised along religious lines, murdered countless people, abducting and raping thousands of women.

In the years following independence, although the British built roads and railways to enable the movement of goods and services, some people still had misgivings about whether Britain developed India or held her back. One thing is for certain: these services opened India to the outside world.

CHAPTER 14

It was becoming increasingly difficult for wealthy Anglo-Indians to remain on their land and pressure was being brought to bear by the Indian government, who had other plans for it. Intercommunal fighting and violence marred the months before and after independence and Birdi noticed a few field hands were not so willing to work for her anymore. Even Nester's most loyal people, who had worked on the estate for years, and their parents before them, now looked at them with contempt. Although they never felt they were in any immediate danger, there was always the chance of some extremist doing them harm.

James was also aware of the situation and as the months passed and more workers left, it became obvious to him Eden was too large to run under-manned. That, together with the mounting feeling of unrest, finally convinced the family to put Eden Estate up for sale.

James and Marie had already started making plans to go to Australia. Eric had married an Indian woman who had no desire to go to Australia as all her family were in Hapur, so they chose to remain in India.

Malcolm was the Headmaster of St. Vincent Hill School in Hapur and his wife Audrey was a teacher; they also decided to go to Australia as there were more opportunities in their profession there. They were not allowed to take any money out of India and as a result James bought furniture, carpets and other household goods, which he had shipped to Australia ahead of time.

A few months after the boys had emigrated, Nester and Birdi received a letter from the Indian government stating there were some 'anomalies' to be addressed before the proceeds of the sale could be released in full, but as a gesture of goodwill they'd enclosed a cheque for twenty per cent of the value of Eden.

The remainder of the proceeds from the sale would be retained by them until those 'anomalies' had been investigated further by their legal department. It was obvious to Nester this was merely a time-wasting exercise on the part of the government and the protracted correspondence, which ensued over the next few years, beat them into submission. They grew tired of the ongoing battles and, following numerous letters from Marie and James asking them to come to Australia, they conceded and emigrated.

When they arrived in Australia they lived with Marie and James, who made sure their parents wanted for nothing, but Birdi had always been a shrewd, independent businesswoman and wasn't used to people making decisions for her, however well intentioned. She also wasn't prepared to sit and do nothing and, following much badgering from Birdi, the family launched their crusade against the Indian government in an effort to have the money released.

Initially, they were informed by the government that they couldn't find any records relating to the sale of the property. It took months and endless correspondence before a letter finally arrived, telling them the money would be transferred to her bank account in Australia within the next seven days. The news was met with jubilation but that was short-lived. After ten days they went to the bank, only to find the remainder of the money was a fraction of the agreed price.

Nester instructed a solicitor to act for the family but after receiving a letter from the Land Registry the solicitor, reading between the lines, suspected that forty years ago when the property was sold some kind of fraud and/or corruption had taken place, since the amount recorded against the sale of Eden was at least one third less than had been agreed upon.

It became apparent this was the reason they'd only released partial funds in the first instance. The solicitor went on to say that whoever had dealt with the sale was now long gone, and it would be counter-productive to pursue the matter further as it would only incur further legal costs and, therefore, erode any proceeds.

They reluctantly accepted his advice and resolved themselves to the fact they'd lost too many years of their lives wrangling with the Indian government. Birdi also appreciated the fact that if it hadn't have been for Nester Freese, her family could have been in a very different situation. They eventually received the residue for the sale of Eden but it was to take nearly forty years.

New Delhi,
1st January 1946.

Now that active hostilities are ended, we can for the first time since 1939 start the New Year with the hope of using it to repair some of the damage caused by war and to begin the building of a new world.

I take this opportunity of thanking everyone who has worked during the war on the staff of War Department, Military Finance, Naval, General and Air Headquarters for the devoted work they have rendered. It has been a record of long and inconvenient hours, and ungrudging personal sacrifice, which all may feel with pride has contributed something to the winning of the war.

This brings you my thanks for all you have done and my good wishes for the New Year.

Auchinleck

General

S/Sgt. Mulvaney, W.G.
P.C.H.

CHAPTER 15

—⁘—

The Passage to Britain

After the independence of India in 1947, life became difficult for Anglo-Indians. By late 1946, the subcontinent was a mess, with British civilians and military officers desperate to leave amidst the growing hostility to their presence among the Indians.

Under British rule, Indians experienced restricted entrance to higher education and the Civil Service, and those Anglo-Indians who held good positions in these sectors were caught in the middle. The Indians treated them with contempt and were envious of them, whilst the gulf between the white community and the Anglo-Indians, whose mixed race caused them to be considered by some as 'impure', was widening.

This growing resentment towards the Anglo-Indians played a major part in their decision to leave India, with many of them accepting the United Kingdom's High Commission's offer of a £10 assisted passage to start new lives in Britain, Canada, Australia and New Zealand. With the mood of unrest which prevailed in many parts of India after the separation, leaving the country was the safest option at the time.

The mass exodus that ensued proved beneficial to the Indian government, which was now able to acquire property and land once owned by the Anglo-Indians for a fraction of what it was worth and, as if to rub salt into their wounds, the Indian government also froze Anglo-Indians' bank accounts, restricting them from taking money out of India.

On 24th November 1949 Bill, Kathleen and their three sons embarked on S.S. Mooltan, leaving Bombay, bound for the United Kingdom – the ship took three weeks to reach Southampton. They were only allowed to take £3 per person out of the country and arrived in Britain with the princely sum of £15 to start their new life.

Kathleen had always had a mortal fear of water since the drowning of her father and dreaded the passage. The listing of the ship made her sea-sick and she counted the days until she would be on terra firma again. It was going to be a long, miserable voyage. She couldn't eat much and even sips of water didn't stay down long. Bill noticed she was losing weight and the black rings under her eyes told him she wasn't sleeping much either.

Although she was ill, Bill still thought she was the most beautiful woman he had ever seen. Her deep brown almond-shaped eyes still smouldered when she looked at him and her smooth, coffee-coloured skin was flawless; he loved her with every fibre of his body.

No: DEL/ E.C./ 36

EMERGENCY CERTIFICATE

THIS IS TO CERTIFY THAT—

..........Mr William, George, Mulvaney..............

has stated to me that he (she) is a

*..................British subject..................

and that I have no reason to doubt his (her) statement.

This Certificate is valid only for the journey

to†....................The United Kingdom

....

‡leaving Bombay on 24th November 1949

...........on the s.s.MOOLTAN

‡for ...the United Kingdom......................,

and must be surrendered to the Immigration Officer at the place of arrival.§

(Signed) ....

(Date)............16th August 1949......

Summary of the statements made by the holder in proof of his (her) British nationality :—

...........................Born at Bandikui, India, on the 27th August 1920.....

Holder financially assisted to proceed from India to the......
United Kingdom by the U.K.High Commissioner in India

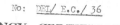

* Insert status.   + Insert British territory of destination.
‡ If the certificate is issued by a Consul at an inland post where the information as to the name of vessel, date of sailing, &c., is not available, it is desirable, in order to avoid possible inconvenience to the traveller on arrival, that the particulars should be added by the British Consular Officer at the port of embarkation, and attested by his consular seal.
§ The possession of this emergency certificate does not exempt the holder from compliance with any immigration regulation in force in the country of destination or from the necessity of obtaining a visa when required.

2156 34455 F.O.P. (4)
P.T.O.

N.R No's SHA. 425889.
SHA. 425886. SHA. 425884. SHA 425 853

72

The holder is accompanied by the following minor children:-

Christian Names	Surname	Place and date of birth	Sex
1. Patrick James	Mulvaney	Peshawar, 20th October 1943	Male
2. Michael George	Mulvaney	Delhi Cantt, 31st December 1944	Male
3. Parnell Leith	Mulvaney	Delhi Cantt, 18th October 1947	Male

SHA. 425887.

SHA. 425888.

SHA. 425886.

By the time they disembarked at Southampton, Kathleen weighed less than seven stone. Bill couldn't bear to see her so pale and thin and that beautiful glow in her skin had now been replaced by an ashen grey colour which gave her a haunted look. My poor, beautiful Katy, he thought – what kind of place have I brought you to?

He thought how helpless she looked with Leith straddled over her hip and Patrick and Michael clinging on to her coat, totally disorientated by the cold and this strange land. They were not equipped for the British weather, especially in January and Bill couldn't help thinking they all looked like refugees as they huddled together in an effort to stay warm. The majority of their clothes were in transit and in any case none of it would have been suitable for the British weather in January.

After they had been cleared by Immigration, they were met by one of Bill's cousins, who took them to his house. It was evident Kathleen and the children were in no fit state to make the last leg of the journey to Scotland, which was another 600 miles. They stayed with Bill's cousin until Kathleen and the children had recovered from the long and arduous crossing.

The room had two double beds pushed closely together and a nightstand. She was so grateful to get her head down somewhere where the bed didn't feel as though it were spinning that she didn't notice how sparsely furnished it was. The boys were cold and tired so she put them into their bed in the clothes they were wearing, including their coats.

She was wakening from her sleep on the veranda in her favourite swing-chair, but when she opened her eyes there was no feeling of sun on her face or her ayah bringing her tea. Instead she felt the coldness of the darkened room and the musty smell of damp linen. She couldn't contain the feeling of overwhelming sadness and buried her face in her pillow and cried like a child. She hadn't cried that way since her father had died when she was twelve, nor could she ever remember her heart ache so badly. She stuffed the corner of the pillow into her mouth to prevent Bill and the children hearing her. The bed shook as she cried and her sobs awakened Bill. He took her in his arms and held her until she'd stopped crying. She missed her mother, her family and her beautiful Eden Estate.

They travelled to Scotland by train and as she looked out of the window she couldn't help thinking how grey everything looked.

The towns they passed had enormous chimneys vomiting out large billows of dark smoke – she thought this must be the reason why they had never seen the sun since they arrived, but in time she would come to realise it wasn't the smoke which hid the sun, it was just that the sun hardly ever came out in Britain in February and the days were very short.

It was early morning and as he looked out of the window of the train, Patrick kept wondering when the sun would come up, but the more north they travelled, the more grey the skies became. All the buildings were grey and most of the towns they passed were ugly in comparison to the beautiful blonde-coloured buildings in India. Here they didn't have fruit trees and fields with guava and melons; instead the trees were bare and nothing grew in the fields – everything looked so barren. He shuddered at the thought of life in such a cold, unwelcoming place.

Patrick was the eldest of the three boys and old enough to realise that this new beginning in Britain was not turning out as he had imagined and an awful emptiness and homesickness swept over him. He wished he was back in India on Eden, where the sun was warm and he was happy. He missed his beautiful home, his Nana, cousins, aunts and uncles.

Patrick moved away from the window and snuggled up to his mother; he loved the way she always smelled of perfume – Elizabeth Arden's Blue Grass, that was her favourite. He felt safe and warm with her arm around him and with the soothing clickety-clack of the train he soon fell asleep and dreamed he was back home in India, walking in the peach groves with Michael and their ayah.

Bill and the two younger boys were on the opposite side of the carriage and Kathleen was thankful that they'd all fallen asleep. She put her head back, gave a long sigh, and surrendered to exhaustion.

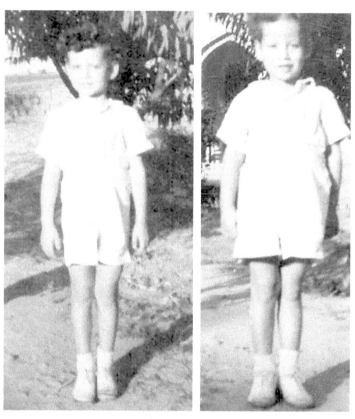

Patrick and Michael under the peach trees

CHAPTER 16

W When they arrived in Lanark they were taken to Bill's aunt's house, where they were shown to a room at the back of the house. The children looked at their mother in bewilderment. She'd promised them it would be better when they got to Scotland – but not only was it colder, but the room was even smaller. Their beautiful brown eyes had lost their sparkle, which had now been replaced by a look of emptiness and sadness. They too were feeling homesick. This was to be their home for the next few months.

The £15 they'd been allowed to bring with them was hardly going to last any time. They would have to accept help from Bill's aunt until Kathleen got a job as a teacher, but that was to prove more difficult than she thought. The only work Bill could find at first was a nightwatchman on a building site.

He had been a bookkeeper for a short while in India after the war, following his discharge from the Army, but it was proving extremely hard to find anything comparable in Scotland. He had written to a former employer in India, who provided him with a reference, but even equipped with this, he was unsuccessful on several occasions when applying for work.

Kathleen was left with the boys most nights and her only company were a few books she had brought with her. They all shared the same room and she would wait until the boys were asleep until she used the small night-light to read. She found escapism through her books and, at least for a while, she'd imagine she was somewhere else other than in this alien existence she had come to know as life.

CHARACTER CERTIFICATE.

Certified that I have known Mr. _W. G. Mulvaney_
son of _J. W. Mulvaney_ for the last _one_ years
_____ months and that to the best of my knowledge and
belief he bears a reputable character and has no antecedents
which render him unsuitable for Government employment.

2.   Mr. _Mulvaney_ is not related to me.

Place _Meerut_   Signature _____

Date _4 Feb 45_   Designation _____

Bill's reference from India

Kathleen sent her resumé to the Education Authority and every day she waited for the letter to come to invite her for interview. The days passed and no letter came. Then, about six weeks later, a brown envelope arrived. She tore the envelope open and started to read. It said that although she was Senior Cambridge educated, her qualifications were not recognised in Britain and, therefore, she would have to sit an examination in this country to be able to teach here. At first she felt deflated but knew it was only a temporary set-back. She felt confident after sitting the exam and was certain it would only be a matter of time before she'd hear from the Education Authority, and she was right. A week later she got a letter from them saying they were sorry but at the present time there were no vacancies but she could re-apply at a later date.

Birdi had drummed into the children that education was paramount and never stopped repeating her mantra in her own inimitable way: 'What's in your head, nobody can take away.' Kathleen had worked so hard to get her qualifications to be a teacher, but the timing was not in her favour since she was forced to leave India before she had her first teaching post.

A few months later she applied again and this time she received a letter saying that there were no teaching positions available but there were vacancies for domestic staff and she could start immediately. The money they had brought with them had gone and even after selling most of her Indian gold they were now completely broke. She had no alternative but to accept what they were offering. She'd never scrubbed floors before and her hands were constantly sore. She couldn't keep up with the other women, most of whom were unkind to her, telling her that if she didn't keep up she'd be better looking for other work. A few of them were kind enough, but it was the others who hurt her most with their comments about her colour. She had never heard women use such foul language before and even though the money helped, she hated it and left after six months.

It was shortly after this that Kathleen told Bill she was going to have a baby. Although money was tight, Bill was delighted. If the baby was a girl, she was to be called Joyce after Kathleen's sister, who died in a plane crash earlier that year.

She had already sold most of her beautiful Indian gold when they first arrived but of course she never got what it should have been worth and now with a baby on the way, she had no choice but to sell the rest of it – even the fabulous piece she was given by her mother on her wedding day.

There had been no choice but to sell her wedding gift from her mother – it broke her heart to part with it, but Birdi knew what Kathleen and Bill were going through; she'd already told Kathleen in a previous letter how bad she felt because she couldn't help out financially, at least not at the moment with the Indian government's ruling regarding the assets of Anglo-Indians.

The family outside Aunt Jean's house

Chapter 17

———⦿⦿⦿———

Kathleen's sister Joyce had met a young radio operator called Robert Espie, who was stationed at Air Transport Command in New Delhi during the war. They were married in New Delhi and shortly afterwards moved to Anchorage in Alaska, where he was attached to the Sixth Radar Unit of the United States Air Force at Elmendorf Air Field and was due to be discharged in six months.

He had purchased several acres of land in Anchorage and was in the process of having a house built for the arrival of their second child.

It was 1950 and Bob and Joyce were looking forward to the birth of their baby. Their little son Victor had been born 20 months ago. Joyce was seven months pregnant and her health wasn't good due to the Alaskan climate. Bob was afraid she may get ill before the baby was born, so he persuaded her to go to Rifle, Colorado to stay with his relatives and have the baby there. At first she was reluctant to go as she didn't want to be away from Bob for such a long time but in the end she agreed, thinking it would be better for Victor as he was suffering from a chest infection and, like her, perhaps he would benefit from a change of climate.

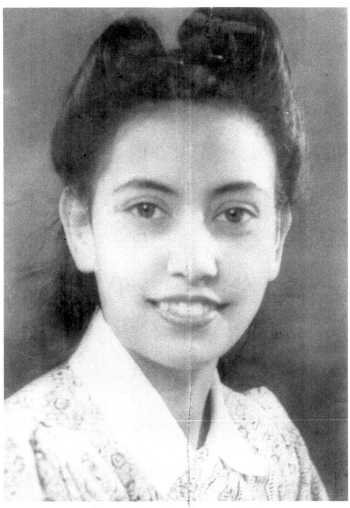

Joyce Merilyn Stanley – aged 20

Worked at Air Transport Command in New Delhi as a telephone operator, where she met Bob

Robert Espie, radio operator at the RCAF (Royal Canadian Air Force) Air Transport Command stationed in New Delhi

Joyce with Bob hours before boarding the C-54 transport carrier

FAMILY CIRCLE IS BROKEN

IT WAS A HAPPIER DAY for the Espe family, when this exclusive picture was taken here in Anchorage last summer. Mrs. Joyce M. Espe, and their 20-month-old son, Victor, were aboard the missing C 54 lost in Yukon country last Jan 26, 15 days ago. Her husband, James R. Espe, hitchhiked from Elmendorf AFB Ft. Richardson, to Whitehorse to join in the search for his family. He has since returned to Anchorage. Mrs. Espe was a resident of India, and met her husband while he was stationed there during the war. Mrs. Espe was on her way to Colorado to have another baby.

Picture taken from the *Anchorage Daily News* dated Monday, January 30th 1950

The C-54 transport carrier plane was scheduled to leave three hours earlier but after a run down the field it failed to take off due to a malfunction of a feathering motor in one of the propellers. A few hours later they were told that the plane had been given the all-clear to resume the flight. The crew had fitted all the passengers with parachutes and Bob's last words to Joyce were: 'If you have to jump, give the baby to Roy.' (He was referring to Sgt Roy Jones who was going to be discharged on arrival at Great Falls in Montana.) They said their goodbyes and Roy promised he would take good care of Joyce and Victor and as the Skymaster taxied down the runway, he could see little Victor smiling and waving from the window of the plane. He never saw his family again.

Telegram dated 8th February 1950 reads:

DEAREST CATHLINE WITH BROKEN HEART MUST SAY MY BELOVED JOYCE AND TWO DEAR BABIES SUDDENLY CALLED HEAVEN DUE AIRPLANE CRASH AIR LETTER FOLLOWS LOVE = BOB

The telegram came in the afternoon; Bill was at work, the older boys were in school and Kathleen was getting Leith dressed to go shopping. When she read it she felt as though her whole world had fallen in on her and she broke down in tears. Leith saw his mother crying and it frightened the child. Kathleen quickly wiped her eyes and pretended there was nothing wrong. She felt her knees weaken and slumped to the floor and held Leith tightly in her arms. She sat on the floor, holding him whilst rocking back and forth and that's where she stayed until the boys found her. The telegram was on the table and Patrick picked it up and read it. He told Michael to take Leith into the living room then sat down beside his mother and put his arms around her – she was so grateful Patrick was there; him being her first-born, the bond had been strong between them. He constantly looked out for her and often demonstrated qualities beyond his years, especially when it came to helping her with the two younger children.

When Bill came home he read the telegram and she could see he was fighting back his tears. He loved Joyce too; she was such a gentle person. Even though they had been thousands of miles apart, they had remained very close and kept in touch by letter on a monthly basis.

The months that followed were difficult for Kathleen and at first it was challenging just getting through each day, but the children depended on her and she knew she had to get on with life for the sake of her family; but the ache she felt didn't subside for years. Each time she looked at Joyce's picture the memories of her came flooding back.

When Bob was informed that the plane was missing, he was granted emergency leave and arrived at Whitehorse on the Saturday. He stayed in the rescue operations room all night and on Sunday morning boarded the first search plane to leave the base. The plane landed at Snag, where the C-54 last made radio contact and Bob made a point of talking to the radio operators who had received the report. They worked out that the aircraft was about 25 miles from Snag and were surprised immediately after they received the transmission from the plane because they believed it had been sent out from a Gibson Girl – a radio set used for emergencies.

HUGE TWO-NAT
SEEKS 44 ON

ANCHORAGE DA

ALASKA'S FASTEST GROWING NEWSPA

VOL. IV, No. 225-D.   Member United Press Associations   ANCHORAGE, ALASKA, MONDAY, JANUARY 30, 195

Congregation Conti
As Fire Sweeps Chu

Furnace Explodes In Baptist
Church During Services

A furnace exploded in the First Baptist Church annex during services yesterday, but while firemen fought stubborn flames, church members prayed next door.

Rev. Felten Griffin shepherded two classes of young folks out of the burning building. "We'll let the firemen fight the fire, and we'll go next door and pray for them," he told the youngsters.

Today the preacher said that as far as he was concerned, the annex, used for class activities, was a total loss. The basement, second floor and outside walls are gutted, and the main floor is burned.

Loss is covered by insurance, Rev. Griffin said.

The fire department has made a tentative estimate of $1500 for damages.

'AMMO' FOR CHRYSLER PICK

Sunday School yesterday, and discovered someone had accidentally picked 'the little gadget stove was still hot, and I told that turns the oil, and that the fire had thus gone out. The group I wasn't about to turn any oil into the hot stove and run the risk of an explosion."

But almost as soon as the minister left, a 'teen age boy, in an attempt to be helpful went about starting the furnace. The re

Headline from the *Anchorage Daily Times* –
Monday 30th January 1950

95

N AIR ARMADA
MISSING C-54

Y NEWS

BIG AERIAL FLEET COMBING CANADA FOR MISSING PLANE: CLEARING WEATHER AIDS HUNT

By CLIFF CERNICK
(ANCHORAGE DAILY NEWS STAFF CORRESPONDENT)

WHITEHORSE, Y.T., Jan. 30 (U.P.) — A two-nation armada spurred on by a determined RCAF officer's "we will find them today," fanned out over frozen sub-Arctic terrain in search of a missing C-54 transport today, despite plunging temperatures and darkening skies.

The missing airforce transport, carrying 44 persons, including a woman and baby son, disappeared Thursday.

Royal Canadian Air Force Commodore M. Costello's optimistic forecast was based on the increasing number of planes in the air, and the narrowing of the search to two "priority areas."

RCAF search squadrons began taking off at 7 a.m. (PST). More U.S. planes joined the RCAF ships every hour as the search was intensified.

The priority areas were set up after residents sent persistent reports of explosions, flares and lights.

One very dangerous area in the immediate vicinity of Whitehorse remained unchecked because of dangerous weather conditions. Lt. Col. E. R. Strause directing search operations for the U. S. Air Force, said this area would be checked later today.

The area from Northway, Alas-

~~~~~~~~~~~~~~~~~
Through the courtesy of the Air Force, NEWS reporter Cliff Cernick has been flown to Whitehorse to cover the search for the missing C-54 for readers of this paper.
~~~~~~~~~~~~~~~~~

ka, to Edmonton, Alta., was being blocked off in 30 square mile grids with planes assigned to each grid.

Commodore Costello admitted

Soldier Joins Search For Wife, Baby

By CLIFF CERNICK

WHITEHORSE, Y. T. — A distraught Army sergeant joined the armada of searchers looking for the missing C-54 transport plane in northern Canada today, hoping and praying he would be the first to sight the downed plane and its survivors.

Sgt. James R. Espe was granted permission to join the combined "Operation Mike" after he hitch-hiked from Elmendorf Field, Anchorage, Alaska, here yesterday. Espes wife and 20-month-old son were aboard

96

After talking to the co-ordinator, Bob learned that he'd thought it strange when there was no word from a plane with four engines and three radios flying in daytime. It was over Snag when the last transmission had been received and at that time it was reported light to moderate winds with slight turbulence.

On Sunday snow fell over Whitehorse for almost eight hours and the RCAF planes circling Carecross were hampered by snowfall which forced them back to base. Temperatures hovered below zero most of the day and then plummeted to 35 below at night. The search area extended from Snag near Alaska's northern border to Great Falls, a distance that stretched from the Atlantic seaboard to the Rocky Mountains and United States. The search for the missing C-54 had now turned into a two-nation task, and 'Operation Mike' was set up. 'Exercise Sweetbriar', the largest para-troop operation ever made in the sub-Arctic, was scheduled to get underway on 13th February and the first of 4,700 U.S. and Canadian troops were already stationed there. Six Canadian and U.S. Air Force 'pararescue' men were placed strategically in the search area at Whitehorse, Watson Lake, Fort Nelson and Edmonton.

RCAF search squadrons began taking off at 7 am. More U.S. planes joined them as the search intensified. The priority areas were set up after residents sent persistent reports of flares and lights in the sky.

The airway from Northway, Alaska to Edmonton, Atlanta was being blocked off in 30-square-mile grids, with planes assigned to each grid. The search was the biggest and most expensive in the history of the northwest. More than 7,000 men were engaged in the operation, which had cost more than $1,000,000 one newspaper reported at the time.

On Monday morning at Great Falls, Montana, more planes began taking off at 15-minute intervals to search 1,250 miles of Yukon wilderness. Already, scores of planes had criss-crossed 55,000 square miles of the far North Country, which included every type of terrain.

The longer the search continued, the more Bob's hope waned. Saturday would have been Joyce's 23rd birthday and Bob had slipped a small box into her luggage as a surprise when she arrived in Colorado. It contained a little silver bracelet with the words *To Mummy with love from Victor x x* engraved on the inside.

On 10th February, almost 15 days after contact was lost with the Skymaster, distress signals were being received near Yukon and the British Columbia border. Teams of operators with special radio sets fanned out across the region but there were no further SOS signals. Major search operations ended shortly afterwards but no wreckage was ever found.

In every letter he wrote to Kathleen, Bob was convinced that the C-54 had put down somewhere and that Joyce was still alive. He re-married many years later and told his daughter Jean all about Joyce. He said he still loved Joyce and if she ever came back he would like them all to live together – he never got over her.

In the months that followed, he wrote to Kathleen almost every week and it was evident Bob had suffered some sort of breakdown. All his letters were the same. He was obsessed with finding the answers to his questions about the disappearance of the C-54, saying he was determined to get the search re-started. Bill knew how hard it was for Kathleen just to get through each day following Joyce's death and the constant stream of letters from Bob had an adverse effect on her recovery. She found the letters distressing and Bill noticed the change in her every time she received one and decided to hide them from her.

CHAPTER 18

———✦☙✦☙✦———

In 1948 the family had moved to a house in Wellgate in Lanark and although they now had two bedrooms, the walls ran with condensation in the winter and the boys were never free of colds owing to the damp conditions.

In February 1954 Kathleen got sick and was admitted to hospital. She had contracted pneumonia due to the damp conditions in the house and lack of proper ventilation. This was an extremely difficult time for Bill. Joyce was three years old and Ian was only one year old. With no parents in this country to help with the children, he was referred to Social Services, who wanted to take the children into care. They told Bill it would be highly unlikely to find a foster home which would take all five of them. Social Services decided the three older boys would be split up and sent to three different foster homes and the two babies would go to Ridge Park Children's Home. The boys were distraught at the thought of being split up and when Bill's Aunt Jean said she would have the boys Bill was more than grateful. At least the boys would be together and Aunt Jean was kind to them.

Patrick, Michael and Joyce at the old house

Bill and Patrick accompanied the social worker when they took Joyce and Ian to the home. Bill had Ian in his arms and Patrick was carrying Joyce. As they walked along the corridor Bill was becoming anxious at the thought of leaving the children when they were so young. He felt he was deserting his children in their time of need and although he knew there was nothing he could do to change the circumstances, it did nothing to ease the guilt he felt.

They were shown into a room with six cots in it. There were no other children in any of the cots and Bill asked if the children would be on their own in this room. He was relieved when the matron assured him that the other little boy and girl who shared the room were having lunch and they would be back later. At least Joyce would have someone to play with.

As he handed his little son over, Bill had to fight his tears back. He had to remain in control and as he turned to take Joyce from Patrick, he could see the tears in his son's eyes. The social worker took Joyce from Bill and took her to the window to show her the birds, which presented the opportunity for Bill and Patrick to slip out without upsetting her. They had only gone a little way down the corridor when they could hear the children crying and calling for them. The sound of their cries was the last thing Bill heard when he went to sleep that night. He felt certain it would be the same for Patrick.

Bill was looking forward to Sunday to take Joyce and Ian out of the home and take them to Castlebank Park to be with their brothers for a while. It felt good to have his family back together again, even just for a short while, but he was already anticipating the heartbreak of leaving them in the home at the end of the day. It proved too upsetting for all the children when they left the two young ones after their day out. No pleasure came from the visit for either Bill or the children. Each time he took them back to the home he came away feeling inadequate and miserable.

After three weeks Kathleen was discharged from hospital. The doctor wrote a letter to the housing department of the Council, advising them that Kathleen could not go back to the house in Wellgate as it would be detrimental to the health of her children, particularly the two younger ones, who would be extremely vulnerable to the damp conditions. Almost immediately, the family were re-located to a brand new five-apartment house in Melvinhall Road on a newly developed council estate.

Bill with the children at Castlebank Park on their Sunday visit

CHAPTER 19

———⚬⟨⚬⟩⚬———

When Bill and Kathleen first arrived in Lanark they had joined the Episcopalian Church of England. At the time, Kathleen thought it might be a way of integrating the family into the small community and every Sunday the family attended church. Each child had one set of school clothes and one set of Sunday best, which Kathleen kept immaculate.

One Sunday after church, Miss Eadie one of the ladies of the congregation came up to her and complimented her on her lovely family, saying they looked as if they had stepped out of a bandbox. She was a retired school teacher who never married and looked forward to catching up with the family on Sundays. Kathleen was so proud of her beautiful children and her very handsome husband, but even as Miss Eadie spoke, Kathleen couldn't supress the feeling of dread which gripped her every Sunday.

She would have to go to the greengrocers and stand in line for the fruit rations for the two younger children and the inevitable outcome of the whole futile operation. She never told Bill why she hated it so much but he knew it was something far more serious than just the end of the weekend with the family – he recalled that he had never seen either Joyce or Ian ever eating the fruit they were supposed to get. After some probing she told him the reason the children never got the rationed fruit was that there was never anything left by the time it came to her turn. He thought this was very strange and told her to do exactly as she always did and that he'd be across the street watching her. When it came her turn, the greengrocer announced the fruit was finished for today and pulled the shutters down. When Kathleen moved along, the shutters miraculously went up again and the greengrocer continued to trade.

Bill saw him pull the shutters back up and was furious. He stormed across the street, grabbed the greengrocer by the throat and demanded the fruit for his two children, which, as he reminded him, they were entitled to as both of them had been born in Lanark and, as such, were British citizens. Some of the women in line cheered Bill – they'd seen the greengrocer do this week after week and had watched Kathleen and her two little children walk away with nothing.

Kathleen had never complained and decided it was best to keep on his good side in the hope that he'd somehow mellow. The other women never spoke up in case they received similar treatment.

After Bill had showed the greengrocer the 'error of his ways', there was never a problem with the fruit rations again, in fact, he would make a special effort to speak to the children, but children – however small – can sense good and bad in people and their instinct told them he was not a good man. They hid behind Kathleen until she'd been served and they could get away from him.

CHAPTER 20

⸻❦⸻

The family were thrilled with their new house. There were four houses in each of the six blocks on the top half of the estate and the middle had been planted with grass, where the children could play. For the first time in a long time, Kathleen felt happy. The children had clean, dry rooms of their own and Bill had a garden to grow his vegetables. After living in the old, damp house it felt almost palatial. It was one of only three five-apartments on the estate. On the ground floor was a living room, kitchen, bedroom and a downstairs toilet. Upstairs there were three large bedrooms and a family bathroom.

Just like Bill and Kathleen, all the families there had recently been re-housed from poor housing and everyone was starting from scratch. One family in the next house but one was Jock and Jessie Frood; they had four children, all similar ages to Kathleen and Bill's children and both families quickly became great friends. This friendship was to last a very long time. At first, Kathleen wondered how the boys would be treated and dreaded the thought of them enduring the same misery they experienced at school but it soon became apparent that these children were different – they were completely oblivious to the boys' colour and it was only a matter of days before they were running around having fun with their new-found friends.

Kathleen – the first day at the new house in Melvinhall Road

Ian and Joyce – a year after moving to Melvinhall

CHAPTER 21

⸻❧❧⸻

1957

Kathleen and Bill rented a Morris Minor to take the two younger children to England to see Bill's mother. His parents had left India in 1950 and settled in the new town of Crawley in Sussex, where his father had died a few years earlier.

Bill constructed a makeshift bed for Joyce at the back of the seats by putting a small upturned crate in each well behind the front seats. He then put a piece of plywood on top of the crates and covered the ply with a heavy folded quilt which functioned as a mattress. Ian was travelling first class with the back seat all to himself.

It was a rare occasion to see a new car in Melvinhall Road in 1957 and most of their friends had gathered round the car.

Joyce's friends Rita and Irene found it fascinating watching Bill preparing the makeshift bed and were longing to try it out. Irene climbed into the back seat while Rita manoeuvred herself on top of the quilt. Bill shook his head and smiled. He was amused to learn that he'd done a good job as it was 'really comfy' and that they wished they were going too.

It was a beautiful summer evening and they set off at dusk. By the time they joined the A1, the children were sleeping – obviously the bed was undeniably 'really comfy'. The journey took a little over fourteen hours, with the occasional stop for a bathroom break. Kathleen had packed sandwiches and two flasks containing drinks for the journey. One had milk for the children and the other was full of strong coffee, which she hoped would help Bill in staying awake. As they drove through the night, every so often she'd put her hand on his when he rested it on the gear stick while they listened to the channel playing easy listening music. Now and then one of their favourites would come on and she'd squeeze his hand gently and they'd both reminisce about the good times in India. Kathleen stayed awake most of the journey, only catnapping now and then – a skill she'd mastered in the days when she'd just come off nightshift when the two little ones were babies.

Bill hadn't seen his mother for two years, since she came to Scotland to visit her sister Jean. The children didn't really know her well but as soon as they arrived his mother embraced them warmly and told them of all the lovely places they would be visiting.

Ian and Joyce on Brighton Pier, eating candyfloss

Ian, Bill, Kathleen and Joyce on holiday in England

Joyce and Ian

Kathleen and Bill

CHAPTER 22

———⁓◦⊙◦⁓———

It was the start of the summer holidays and the boys were helping John (Jock's son) to erect a ten-man tent in which the boys proposed to have a sleepover. The other children watched as the boys pulled up the main pole and secured the guy ropes to the pegs and as soon as it was up everybody ran inside and bagged a spot. Not to be outdone, the girls decided to do something similar, but they didn't have a real tent. They had to fashion something out of old sheets, washing ropes and pieces of sticks hammered through the sheets into the ground. Once it was up, the girls went inside to prepare their 'accommodation' for the night.

The boys waited a short time. John quietly went to the front of the makeshift tent and Michael went to the back. Leith mouthed the words 'one, two, three', and on the count of three, both boys pulled out the main pegs supporting the clothesline over which the sheets had been draped and the whole thing fell on the girls. It was one of those warm summer evenings when most of the mothers had come out to be with the children and when the 'tent' fell on the girls, the mothers were beside themselves with laughter as they watched the girls getting more and more entangled as they writhed around trying to free themselves.

Nobody locked their doors, everyone helped each other and the only time the colour of her skin was mentioned was when the other women gave Kathleen compliments.

Kathleen had missed the company of women her own age and enjoyed the summer evenings after tea, when the mothers came out and chatted while the children played. The house had been built on a corner plot, where Bill had planted vegetables. Most evenings after work, he could be found in the garden tending the vegetables.

Kathleen preferred vegetable curries to meat so he made sure he planted plenty of peas, potatoes and onions as well as Brussels sprouts and carrots for winter. Some of the smaller children would peer through the fence and ask him what he was growing and when he told them he was growing Golden Wonder potatoes, one of them replied that she'd come back when they had grown into crisps! He couldn't help but laugh – it felt good to belong somewhere – he liked the people here but most of all, he saw something in Kathleen that had been missing for a long time: her beautiful smile.

Bill and Kathleen at a New Year's dance

The majority of young mothers at the time stayed at home and looked after their children and those who did work usually did so on a part-time basis since they needed to be home when the children came out of school. Jessie was a great friend to Kathleen and together, with the help of Patrick, things had a way of working themselves out during the holidays.

Jessie would organise walks for the children to the Clyde River and the children would take a picnic with them – usually jam sandwiches, crisps and bottles of fizzy drinks. She would be at the front of the procession with the children following on; sometimes there would be as many as fifteen. The older children would each be responsible for two or three of the younger ones on the way down to the swimming hole. They'd set off, resembling little ducklings following their mother.

All the children learned to swim at a very early age and if they couldn't swim when they went down to the river they certainly could when they came back. One part of the river had created a natural pool which the locals had named the Heart because of its distinctive shape. The pool was about six feet deep in the middle, but the part which looked like the point of a heart was only about three feet deep and it was in this part of the pool the younger children learned to swim by being thrown in by the older ones! It truly was a case of sink or swim. This ritual had been going on for years and was never carried out unless there was an adult present and at least two of the older boys, who were excellent swimmers. They would stand in the pool to ensure that the learner didn't get near the middle.

Joyce and Ian on the bridge to the 'Heart'

No one was ever in danger and the learners were made aware of what would happen to them on their initiation and, at that point, had the chance to decline – but no one ever did. It was always great fun on initiation day and strangely enough, the dupes appeared to enjoy it immensely because they entered the water with a huge grin on their faces. It was difficult to determine if this was an expression of glee or hysteria.

In the summer some of the older children found work in the strawberry fields in the Clyde Valley and in the October school week holiday they worked on Mr Brown's farm, lifting potatoes. This was preferable to picking strawberries as Mrs Brown would bring sausages, mashed potatoes and two big jugs of gravy to the barn at lunchtime. The barn had an old table and a couple of wobbly chairs. Bales of straw had been placed around it to accommodate the workers, who included some of the mothers, who made sure everyone was doing their fair share. The furrows were marked out in 'stints' using two sticks about a foot high and spaced twenty-five feet apart.

Once all the potatoes in the 'stint' had been lifted, the markers were moved to the next furrow. A few of the boys thought they'd be clever, shortening the length of their stint by moving the markers closer together when they moved to the next furrow, therefore lifting less potatoes.

Mr Brown had seen this prank being pulled many times and was well prepared for this. The offenders were given a choice of having their wages docked or not being entitled to Mrs Brown's bangers, mash and gravy at lunchtime. It didn't seem to matter to the boys that they'd have been working for nothing all morning because when it came to the choice between nutritional value and monetary value, the bangers and mash won. After all, it was one of the main reasons for working at the 'tatties'.

Mr Brown's tried-and-tested remedy for deterring malingerers had achieved the desired effect. He knew the children relied on the money and often doubted whether he could actually bring himself to dock anybody's wages.

CHAPTER 23

—◦⟨◎⟩◦—

Bill and Kathleen were pondering over what to get Joyce for her birthday. She loved animals and could usually be found across the road, watching Mr Mann taking care of his rabbits. The Manns were an older couple who didn't have children and who, for the most part, kept themselves to themselves. In the summer, Mr Mann would take the rabbits out of their hutches and put them in a large run which he'd constructed using a wooden frame covered with chicken wire.

Joyce had never seen rabbits like these before. They were jet-black and totally unlike the usual English Chain rabbits which could be bought at any pet shop. She asked her parents if she could have one and Bill and Kathleen consented, since the quandary of what to get her had been solved.

Bill made a hutch which he placed on legs three feet off the ground to deter predators. The leftmost quarter of the structure would be where the rabbit would sleep. The rest of the hutch was given over to create space where Bobby could exercise. Joyce was proud of the new hutch her father had built and it wasn't long before news got round and her friends came round to meet Bobby.

A few months later, Joyce's friend Irene was going on holiday and asked her if she would look after her rabbit and it was agreed she would bring it round in the morning before they left. She put her rabbit into the cage and the girls watched, tentatively hoping they wouldn't fight as they were both males. They were relieved when both rabbits settled down in the exercise area and seemed quite content in each other's company.

About a month after Irene had taken her rabbit back Joyce went out to feed Bobby and was distressed to see he had pulled a lot of his fur out and appeared lethargic, as he was usually out in the run waiting for his food. She picked him up to investigate further and saw eight newborn baby rabbits curled up in a nest which was lined with the fur Bobby had pulled out.

She ran into the house excitedly, announced that Bobby was a girl and promptly ran back out to the hutch. Bill and Kathleen looked at each other in bewilderment and went to see what all the fuss was about. Bill lifted the top of the hutch to reveal the newborn kits and told Joyce not to touch them until they were at least four weeks old.

Joyce went out to tell her friends and as soon as they saw the kits they all wanted one. Bill told the children that they would have to ask their parents first and also that they wouldn't be able to take them from their mother until they were eight weeks old. It wasn't long before Melvinhall became a hive of industry, building rabbit hutches.

CHAPTER 24

———◦⟨ᴖⱺ⟩◦———

Bellfield had ceased to be a sanatorium for patients with tuberculosis and was now a hospital for children with special needs. Some of the children suffered from severe autism and others from Down's Syndrome. Kathleen had completed the necessary courses to enable her to work with these children and whilst some days could be challenging she found tremendous job satisfaction due to the varied nature of the children's needs.

The children loved her. When she came on duty they would run to her and cuddle her – sometimes in their excitement nearly knocking her off her feet. There was one beautiful little girl who had Down's Syndrome called Lucy, whom Kathleen was particularly fond of. Lucy was continually drawing people and she drew a picture of Kathleen and was eager to give it to her when she came onto the ward.

She handed Kathleen a piece of folded paper and when she opened it up she felt a lump in her throat. Lucy had drawn Kathleen in her uniform with a halo above her nurse's hat – she went on to explain that it was Kathleen and that she was her 'brown angel'. Kathleen was smiling and thanking Lucy for the beautiful picture when one of the ambulance drivers came running into the ward, telling Kathleen that there had been an accident and she would have to come right away. She followed him out of the gate and saw his partner kneeling beside Joyce, and Joyce's friend Annette standing crying.

Annette explained that they'd taken Leith's go-kart to Bellfield Hill, but when they set off down the hill she became frightened as the kart was going too fast and she jumped off. She told them how it had crashed through the fence, crossed the road and broke up when it hit the wall of Bellfield Hospital. Kathleen could see her daughter was semi-conscious and bleeding from the left side of her head. She was trying to speak but her speech was slurred and incoherent.

Kathleen knew that with any serious head injury the next forty-eight hours would be crucial. Joyce was rushed to hospital, where it was confirmed she had a fractured skull and had to have the wound stitched. When Bill and Kathleen left the hospital that evening Joyce's speech had not improved and Bill was becoming concerned. Kathleen had seen enough head injuries to reassure him that this was normal and that he would see a major improvement in the morning, but neither of them got much sleep that night.

On the second day after being admitted, Joyce sat up and asked if anyone was taking care of her rabbits. Kathleen and Bill were elated to hear her speak again and reassured her that all eight of them were thriving. Later that day at evening visiting, Leith came with their parents to see Joyce. He bent close to her and took a jet-black baby rabbit from his pocket and placed it on her bed. As Joyce held it, she said it felt like black velvet and held it to her cheek. Kathleen was annoyed that he'd brought the rabbit into the ward but when she saw the effect it had on Joyce, she forgave him and even helped to conceal it from the other patients. The next day Joyce was discharged.

She couldn't wait to see the rabbits. They were now six weeks old and all her friends had chosen the one they wanted. Not that they could ever be sure if they would receive the one of their choice as five of them were black and the other three were a grey-blue. Nevertheless, hutches had been built and were awaiting the precious cargo.

It was Sunday morning and the family were getting ready to go to church. Joyce had gone out to feed the rabbits and came rushing in, screaming and crying. Bill couldn't make out what she was saying and he ran out to see what was wrong. He couldn't believe the carnage before him. All nine rabbits had been slaughtered. Blood was running down the outside of the hutch and body parts were strewn all over the run. He knew it hadn't been a fox because the wire mesh was still intact – the top and bottom bolts had been slipped and he suspected that a ferret had been put in for the sport. He knew of a couple of families that kept ferrets but they lived in the other part of town. Nobody from the adjacent streets would have carried out such a senseless act of cruelty. Bill was so intent on clearing out the dead rabbits he never noticed the red spray paint on the coal cellar wall which read – 'DARKIES GO HOME'.

Joyce was inconsolable. Bill told Kathleen to take her to Jessie's house to avoid her being subjected to further grief when he was disposing of the animals and dismantling the hutch. There was also the job of painting over the graffiti on the coal cellar wall.

CHAPTER 25

Kathleen and her sisters Naomi and Barbara kept in touch on a regular basis, sharing their news in letters, in which they exchanged photographs of their respective children. Naomi wrote to tell Kathleen she had met someone literally by accident.

Naomi had three children all under the age of five – two boys and a girl. Her then husband, John Brien, was a hedonist who rarely worked and depended on his looks to get him by. He spent most of his time loafing around with his friends and felt no contrition in allowing Naomi to provide for him and his children. Birdi never grew tired of telling her how lazy he was and that she'd be better off without him, but in Naomi's eyes he could do no wrong.

Kathleen's youngest sister Barbara was happily married to James Ramsbotham, who she'd been introduced to by one of his friends at a New Year's dance. At the time, he was serving in the Indian Air Force and had come to Delhi to represent his division in the Inter-Services Athletic meet.

Barbara had been an air hostess for a short time before taking her training as a nurse. When James left the Air Force they moved to Tambrah in Madras, where Jim's family livedm but it soon became apparent that the living wage in the south of India was not comparable to that in the north. They now had two children to support, so they moved back to Delhi, where Jim secured a position in Security with the British High Commission. He worked there until 1966, when the family emigrated to England and settled in Thornton Heath, where he worked as a civilian in the police.

Jim and Barbara with Charlotte and Norman

Barbara and Jim at farewell party before leaving for
England in 1966

CHAPTER 26

⸺❧⸺

Naomi was working for the Caterpillar Tractor Company in Delhi as a secretary and looking forward to her promotion, which was due to commence the following month. At last things were going right for her and she envisaged the possibility of a different life for her and the children, but all that was to change. She had only been in her post for two months as a personal assistant when she discovered she was pregnant.

When their twin girls were born, John Brien went to visit Naomi and his daughters in hospital and that was the last time she saw him. Although she was devastated by the situation she now found herself in, she returned to work after a few months following the birth of the twins and it wasn't long after this she had her accident.

Naomi with John and Karen at Eden Estate

One morning, as she was desperately trying to get to work on time, she ran across the road but her mind was on other things. Would the babies miss her as much as she'd miss them? How would she cope with five small children? This was all going through her head – she didn't see the limousine at it rounded the corner and knocked her down. All she could remember was the car was black and was chauffer-driven.

When she woke up she was told she was going to be alright and that she'd only incurred minor abrasions but that she'd been unconscious when brought in. After the nurse left she looked round the room, which didn't look like any hospital she'd been in. Firstly, it had an en-suite and she wasn't sharing the room with anyone else and secondly, the standard of furniture and drapes was far superior to those in a general hospital.

She called the nurse and asked her who was paying for all this and the nurse assured Naomi it had all been taken care of and there was nothing to worry about.

She lay back against her pillows and tried to recall the events which brought her here, but before she could make any sense of it, she felt herself drifting into sleep.

Later that evening the nurse showed two men into the room. The man in the grey cap was obviously a chauffeur and he was holding a large bouquet of flowers. The other man looked to be in his mid-forties and immaculately dressed in a very expensive-looking black suit. He nodded in the direction of the bedside table. The chauffer obediently laid the flowers on the table and stood back. The man in the black suit introduced himself as Norman Shircore and told her that he'd come to offer his apologies for knocking her down but also to reassure her that all medical expenses would be paid for him and all she had to do was to get well. He was soft-spoken with light green eyes and jet-black hair and had an accent which sounded American mixed with something else which she couldn't quite detect.

He was about twenty years older than her and very unassuming, she thought, for someone of his obvious status and as he was recalling the details of the accident, she was no longer listening to what he was saying and was aware she was feeling something other than gratitude. She had never met anyone like him before.

Three days later she was discharged from hospital and when she got home there was a hand-delivered notelet on the mat. It was from Norman, asking her out for dinner. As she read it, she couldn't believe that such a man could conceivably be interested in her. Her excitement soon faded as she realised she couldn't possibly accept his offer: they were so different on so many levels. What would she have in common with such a man? He was obviously well educated and wealthy and was much older than her. What would they talk about? Why was she even thinking like this if she wasn't going to meet him? Nevertheless, she couldn't get him out of her mind so she picked up the phone and called him to say she'd be delighted to join him and he could pick her up at eight the next day.

Now she had to decide what to wear. It hadn't to be anything revealing but yet not too demure and the little black dress – which every woman has in her wardrobe for such occasions – was the discernible choice. She accessorised the dress with a pearl necklace and matching earrings. The whole look was completed by a black clutch bag and black patent leather ankle strap shoes. She looked at herself in the mirror and was pleased with her reflection – she had managed to get her figure back reasonably quickly after the birth of the twins.

The car picked her up promptly at eight and they were driven to Karim's, one of the top restaurants in Delhi. When they walked into the restaurant, it became clear that Norman came here frequently. The maître d' greeted them as they entered, then showed them to his 'usual table'. She needn't have worried about what to talk about and found it surprisingly easy to relax in his company. Naomi decided to be open with him regarding her current situation with John Brien and the children. He sat quietly and listened as she told him how she had been left with five children and, at the present time, her children's wellbeing was paramount. He agreed with her entirely.

She wanted to hear about him and, like her, he wanted to be honest regarding his situation right from the start. He told her that he was divorced from his wife and she now lived in England with his daughter, who was just a few years younger than Naomi. He was the Managing Director of Massey Ferguson and lived in Defence Colony.

A few months passed and the inevitable happened: Naomi fell in love with Norman. He was such a kind, gentle person who treated her like a lady, but she was apprehensive about their future together not just because of her five children, but the age gap between Norman and herself.

Norman asked if he could meet the children and invited her to come to lunch and bring the children. He had answered her inner fears and she knew then he felt the same about her.

Naomi

Norman meeting Naomi's children at the house in Defence Colony.
From left to right: Teresa, Shane, Karen, John and Cecelia

Norman and Naomi with the five children, two months before the family left for Britain

Norman Elliot Shircore had been a Colonel in the British Army and after his discharge he moved into a beautiful home in Defence Colony, an affluent locality situated in south Delhi which had been built for ex-defence servicepeople.

The children liked Uncle Norman from the outset. It was shortly after meeting the children that he suggested that Naomi and the children should live with him instead of the apartment. He pointed out that the house was too big for him anyway and the children would have a garden to play in.

They remained together for the rest of their lives and even though Norman brought the children up as if they were his own, they always referred to him as Uncle Norman.

CHAPTER 27

---◦⌒◦⌒◦---

The older boys had been enrolled in the local primary school and things were very difficult for them. It was 1954 and in Lanark, the small town where Bill and Kathleen had settled, they were the only 'darkies' the other children had ever seen. School was a harrowing experience for the three older boys but they never told their parents about the hurtful taunts and bullying that had now become part of their daily life.

Kathleen had taught them that toughness was a quality of the mind, to have a sense of tolerance and never to raise your hands to anyone. Patrick tried to follow the teachings of his mother but he soon came to realise the children at school took this as weakness and although turning the other cheek would have been the answer in India, it certainly wasn't the case here, and decided to fight back.

At night he would teach his brothers the art of self-defence by any means foul or fair and the three brothers soon gained a reputation as the hard guys in school. Kathleen wasn't fully aware of what was happening to them at school because they hid everything from her to keep her from worrying about them. She knew nothing of the bullying and taunts but she suspected what they may be going through, since she had experienced some hostility when she went food shopping. Patrick, who was ten when he left India, still remembered vividly how his life was back there and hated the street fighter he'd become. Michael and Leith, however, revelled in the reputation they had acquired as 'tough guys'.

Patrick teaching Michel and Leith the 'art of self-defence'
(with Ian, age 3)

CHAPTER 28

---•⊙⊙⊙•---

Kathleen was working three nights a week as an Auxiliary Nurse in Bellfield Sanatorium, which in the 1950s was a hospital for TB patients. In the early years she depended heavily upon the help from Patrick when she came from work in the morning. He helped to get his brothers ready for school while she made breakfast. After the boys had left she would lie in front of the fire so the two little ones didn't go near it – she never slept until noon, when she would get up and make lunch for the children. After they had lunch she would take them upstairs with her and sometimes they'd sleep for a few hours. When the boys came home from school they would look after Joyce and Ian until Bill came home and took over.

She worked in Bellfield Hospital until Joyce and Ian were in primary school. The hospital was just a ten-minute walk from home and she had to pass a construction site to go down the hill to the hospital. She had taken a week's holiday to be with the children during their school summer holidays and was taking Joyce and Ian with her to the hospital to collect her pay.

As she passed the building site some of the men tiling the roofs began to wolf-whistle at her. This had become an everyday occurrence when she walked to work. She simply ignored them, kept her head down and walked past as if she hadn't heard them. She kept walking as usual but Joyce looked up at her and asked why the men were whistling at her. Kathleen asked the children not to say anything to their father because she was afraid of any reprisals Bill may have for the builders. He had seen the way some men looked at her and, although he never showed it, there was a definite underlying feeling of jealousy.

Kathleen with Ian

Now that the two youngest were in school, Kathleen decided to take her training as a State Registered Nurse in Law General Hospital, but it would be a full-time day job and she would need Bill and Patrick's help.

Occasionally Bill would put a bet on a horse and when he lost, money would be tight. Kathleen had to be sure this wasn't going to be something she would be worrying about while she was studying, doing a full-time job and bringing up five children at the same time. Patrick and Michael had jobs on a milk-round and Leith had found himself a paper-round but even with their help, it was a struggle to feed and clothe five children.

When money was tight, they would eat rice, egg curry, dhal and chapattis, but the children now preferred British food and on these occasions Bill had to remind them that if they didn't eat it they would go hungry. He hated to see food being wasted, remembering all the times he had to go without when he was young and the nights he couldn't sleep because of his hunger.

He was as good as his word. He kept his promise and never gambled again. He took over the shopping and the cooking and on Kathleen's days off she would do the laundry for the seven of them, which took up most of the day.

The aluminium boiler had to be pulled out of the workman's press then filled with water several times to wash all the loads, then the mangle had to be screwed onto the deeper of the two sinks to wring the clothes out. It was at times like this she missed the servants.

CHAPTER 29

⁓◦◦⊙◦⊙◦⁓

In 1963 Kathleen graduated as a State Registered Nurse and within six months of passing out, she was made the Sister of Ward 1 in Law Hospital. Ward 1 was the most prestigious ward to get and she could hardly wait to tell Bill. The only thing that marred the celebrations that evening was the write-up in the local paper, where she was referred to as the 'first non-white' to ever hold the position of Sister in Law Hospital. It was still all about colour, she thought, and not about achievement.

Miss Ballantyne, the matron of Law Hospital, had come to admire and respect Kathleen for having achieved so much in the face of adversity and, although she could never be sure, Kathleen thought the matron had a soft spot for her. She put Kathleen forward to represent Law Hospital in a speech-making contest, which she won.

Later that year she was nominated for the Nurse of the Year award and although she didn't win it she still felt honoured to have been nominated.

Kathleen outside Ward 1, Law Hospital

CHAPTER 30

After three years in the general hospital Kathleen started work in the local maternity hospital, where she qualified as State Certified Midwife and in 1964 she took up the position of District Nurse in the small village of Lesmahagow, about 12 miles outside Lanark. She lived in the District Nurse's house on a council estate and was subjected to verbal abuse about her colour. She never told Bill; there was no point – she had been seconded for six months as part of her midwifery course and had to complete this. She had experienced this more than once, especially in the early days when she first arrived in Britain, but on the whole she'd now felt accepted. She had to get on with the job she was there to do and hoped that when people realised she was there to help, they too would accept her.

Eventually some of the mothers got to know her. Kathleen's gentle nature and caring ways had won them over and they looked forward to her visits, although there were still a few families on the council estate that wouldn't even let her in to their homes. Some of the older boys would taunt her and call her a darkie, and on those occasions she found it difficult not to count the days to get back to her family and friends.

It was a bleak place indeed. All the fences had been made using one-inch-square aluminium mesh, popular in council estates in the 1950s. When the wind blew through the mesh it made an eerie noise which made the place seem even more desolate.

Joyce missed her mother desperately. She was at that difficult age, no longer a child but not yet a woman and she missed not having her mother around to talk to. Bill would take Joyce and Ian to Lesmahagow on a Sunday to see their mother and have dinner with her, but this particular Sunday he couldn't take them because the car had broken down. Joyce pleaded with her father to let her go on the bus, saying she hadn't seen her mother for a week and though Bill was reluctant to let her travel on her own, he knew how much she was missing her mother. After pleading with him, he allowed her to go on her own and in any case, the driver was a colleague so he felt sure he would look out for her.

She wanted to show her mother her new powder-blue jacket she'd bought from her catalogue. She worked in a local café at the weekends and Kathleen allowed her to keep what she earned to buy the latest fashions from the catalogue in return for good grades in school.

She could hardly contain her excitement at seeing her mother again and as she sat looking out of the window of the bus she could almost smell the Blue Grass perfume her mother would be wearing.

Lesmahagow was a very small village and the Sunday service was limited to one bus an hour so when it came in, there was only a fifteen-minute turnaround during which time the driver could use the facilities in the public convenience across the road.

As the bus pulled up she noticed some boys waiting for it to stop. As she stepped down from the bus one of the boys asked her where she thought she was going and blocked her from getting off the bus, he called her a darkie, spat on her, punched her in the face then poured a bottle of Coca-Cola over her head. The contents ran down her back and stained her new blue jacket.

When the driver came back he told the boys to leave or he would call the police. He convinced Joyce it would be better if she stayed on the bus and came back to Lanark. She had no choice: if she had tried to get to her mother's house, she'd probably have been beaten up or worse, so she took his advice and went back to Lanark.

When Joyce didn't show up for lunch, Kathleen phoned Bill to see if she was coming and when he told her she'd got the 12:30 bus, Kathleen started to panic. She phoned Bill every fifteen minutes to see if he had heard anything. He told her not to worry and that he'd go to the office at the bus stance and wait for the bus to come in.

He hadn't been waiting long when the Lesmahagow bus pulled in. The driver got out and took Joyce to Bill and told him what had happened. When they got home he phoned Kathleen to let her know Joyce was safe, but when the boys saw the state she was in, it was all Bill could do to keep them from getting on the next bus to Lesmahagow. Bill explained it would only make things worse for their mother and they should forget it and just be thankful that Joyce's injuries weren't any worse. But they didn't forget what had happened to their sister that day and vowed to avenge her.

CHAPTER 31

By now the three older boys had grown up and found careers of their own. Patrick had gone to London and joined the Metropolitan Police. Michael left home when he was sixteen and joined the Royal Navy and Leith had just started an apprenticeship as a joiner with one of the local firms.

Joyce was now sixteen and, just like her mother, she loved to dance and listen to music. The Memorial Hall in Lanark attracted great live bands on Saturday nights and people came from everywhere to hear them play. Joyce had taken her mother's looks and had what her art teacher had once referred to as 'exotic looks', which pleased her greatly since she thought her mother was the most beautiful woman in Lanark.

Marmalade, one of the top groups in the 1960s, was coming to Lanark Memorial Hall – better known as 'The Memo'. The venue always attracted great bands, some of whom became very famous. The place was packed and finding somewhere to dance was proving difficult for Joyce and her best friend Annette. After being jostled around a bit, they decided to take a break and cool off. They bought two Cokes and sat at the side of the dancefloor, watching some people attempt the Hippy Hippy Shake, to which Annette remarked that most of them resembled the dancers in the American films who were always out of time as they tried to imitate the London scene.

They were laughing and chatting when Joyce stopped laughing and suddenly froze. That's when she recognised him. It was her attacker from Lesmahagow. Her heart started thudding as he walked towards her; she wondered what he might do – maybe he'd call her names again or spit on her – but when he asked her to dance, she realised he didn't recognise her now that she was all grown up. She accepted his offer and as they danced she hatched her plan to exact her revenge.

He told her his name was John and that he'd come in from Lesmahagow especially to see Marmalade and as the night wore on she was absolutely certain he still didn't recognise her.

When she told Annette who he was, she was more than willing to be part of the plan. When John asked Joyce if he could walk her home she agreed, but before they left she told Annette to go on ahead and divulge the plan to her brothers.

As they walked, she listened to him boasting about being the toughest man in Lesmahagow and how nobody could ever touch him. He was a thug when he was young and a thug now – he had to be taught a lesson. All she had to do was get him to the back door of her house, where Michael, who was home on leave from the Navy, and Leith were waiting behind the door. The plan was that she was to call out to her mother that she was home and that she'd be in soon. That would be the signal for her brothers to open the door and come outside.

She got to the back door and called to her mother; when the door opened her brothers dragged him into the garden. They asked him to apologise to their sister for what he had done to her. He looked scared and replied that he hadn't done anything to her – he'd just walked her home. Then Joyce reminded him of that day at the bus station in Lesmahagow; she saw his eyes widen in horror and as her brothers led him off, she could hear him crying, saying he was sorry and pleading with them not to hurt him. She felt no guilt, only satisfaction that both she and her mother had been avenged.

CHAPTER 32

———⟨◦⟩———

When her six months had been completed in Lesmahagow, Kathleen went back to the maternity hospital in Lanark. She worked there for one year then returned to Law Hospital, where Bill had been working since 1967.

Bill had qualified as an Operating Department Practitioner, assigned to 'A' Theatre. He always felt he was meant for something other than driving buses but didn't know what, since all he'd ever known was Army life. Kathleen was convinced he was capable of so much more. His military conduct had been described as 'exemplary'. He was highly organised, practical and punctual with good common sense. She reminded him of the qualities he possessed and with a little encouragement he'd taken her advice and completed his three years' training.

As an ODP, Bill was responsible for preparing a range of specialist equipment and drugs such as the anaesthetic machines and intravenous equipment. He also had to prepare other complex machinery like microscopes and endoscopes. During the surgery he worked alongside the surgeons, passing them the correct surgical instruments for the operation in hand and had to be able to concentrate for long periods of time. When the operation was over, it was his responsibility to ensure all surgical instruments and equipment were sterilised and counted swabs disposed of correctly.

He was also the go-between from the surgical team to other parts of the hospital, ensuring each team had everything they needed to carry out the surgery. 'A' Theatre was a busy one and at last Bill had found something to give him some pride in what he did. He hadn't had that sense of belonging since he was in the Army and it felt good to be part of a team again – he too had found his vocation in life.

He was well liked at the hospital and made many friends. He was held in high regard by the surgeons on the team because of his attention to detail and the strong work ethic they had witnessed when they worked alongside him. His sense of order and precision came naturally to him and he attributed these qualities to his life in the Army and was proud to have left the Army with an exemplary record. He also had beautiful handwriting which many of his colleagues remarked upon, but the secret of where he learned it remained so until the latter years of their marriage, when he eventually told Kathleen what had happened to him when he stayed with the Christian Brotherhood.

2   (This page should be entirely free from erasure.)

Final Assessments of Conduct and Character on Leaving the Colours.

Military Conduct _Exemplary._

Testimonial _A conscientious and thoroughly reliable warrant officer whose work and conduct have been maintained at a consistently high standard throughout his service. He has initiative, tact, judgement and a sound sense of loyalty and responsibility. Honest and completely trustworthy._

The above assessments have been read to the soldier.

Signature of Soldier on
Transfer to Reserve
or on Discharge
(Delete words which are inapplicable.)

Place **HASTINGS**

Date **-9 DEC 1948**

O.C. R.A.S.C. A C C

Signature and Rank

Excerpt from Regular Army Certificate of Service

170

CHAPTER 33

1967

Kathleen received a letter from Naomi, telling her they'd decided to come to Britain to live but they couldn't take the children to England until both of them found work and a suitable house within their budget for a family of seven. Naomi asked if the children could stay in Scotland with them until she and Norman had secured jobs and found a house. Although Kathleen's three oldest boys had already left home, it was still going to be crowded with seven children and two adults. Furthermore, because of the different ages of the children it would be inappropriate for them to share rooms. However, after much planning and discussions of how to accommodate the children, it was agreed it could be done and the children arrived in Scotland on 15th January.

Bill picked them up from the airport a little after five o'clock in the afternoon. The temperature was 2 degrees and it had already been dark for two hours. The children sat in complete silence for most of the journey, looking out of the window, commenting only occasionally on what they saw as they passed through the towns. Naomi and Norman had left eight weeks earlier and had secured jobs in Croydon but it was proving difficult to find a suitable home in the London Borough within budget for a large family.

The twins, Theresa and Cecelia, clung to each other in the seat behind Bill while Karen and Shane occupied the other side of the seat. John, the oldest of the five, sat passenger and Bill tried to make conversation with him on the journey to Lanark but John remained silent. On their arrival, they were met by Kathleen, Joyce and Ian and although they were family none had ever met each other before. Kathleen embraced each child in turn and introduced them to Joyce and Ian, who then took them upstairs to show them where they would be sleeping. Their trunks hadn't arrived yet but Kathleen had bought each child flannelette pyjamas, which she'd placed at the bottom of their beds.

All seven children sat round the table and Bill made a safe choice and served them Heinz tomato soup. He knew nothing of their dietary preferences but he hadn't come across a child yet who didn't like Heinz tomato soup, especially in the winter. Ian reached over and helped himself to a piece of crusty bread, then looked at Shane while holding the bread up and proceeded to dip it into his soup. Shane took a piece of bread, looked at Ian and with a playful smile, dipped his bread into the soup, then they both put the bread into their mouths at the same time and proceeded to eat the soup. Bill was happy when he saw the others reaching for the bread and imitating Shane. Their bowls were promptly emptied and replaced by Kathleen's home-made doughnuts and a jug of milk. After supper, the children went into the living room to watch television and it wasn't long before the twins, who were cuddled up to Karen, began to yawn. It had been a long and eventful journey for them and Kathleen was thankful the three girls had fallen asleep so quickly when she had gone back in to check on them. She switched off the light and quietly closed the door.

The boys were watching television and Kathleen and Joyce went into the kitchen to help Bill clear up. After the dishes were put away, they sat round the table and discussed strategy.

Naomi's children would be attending St. Mary's School and Joyce and Ian would be going to school a different route: to Lanark Grammar. Annette, Joyce's best friend, attended St. Mary's School and, if she agreed, she could take them to school and bring them home. Joyce went to Annette's house to ask if she would be willing to take it on and, of course, Annette said she would. The next thing on the agenda was to take the children shopping for winter clothes, coats and boots, with the money Naomi had sent for the children's necessities, prior to starting school.

On Monday Kathleen and Bill took the children to St. Mary's School. As they approached the school gates Kathleen felt the twins' hands tighten around hers. She bent down and assured the girls they would be alright and Theresa responded with a weak smile. After enrolment, they were introduced to their respective teachers and shown the classrooms they would be in the following week.

Bill felt sorry for the children and hoped their time at school would not be a repetition of what the boys went through when they first came to Lanark. He needn't have worried though as the children were welcomed by the other children in their respective classes and made friends quickly. Thankfully, times had changed somewhat over the last eighteen years; that, coupled with the fact that everyone knew they were cousins of the Mulvaneys, meant Naomi's children were very seldom subjected to bullying or racist comments.

The children's four black metal trunks arrived two weeks later, each clearly marked with their names. Bill put two in Ian's room and the other two in the girls' room. Joyce and Ian had never seen trunks like these before; they were like mini wardrobes. When stood up on end, they opened in the middle to reveal a rail on which their dresses and jackets hung; the lower quarter of the trunk housed sweaters and shoes. The inside was lined with fuchsia-pink satin and the smell from the camphor balls was exceptionally pungent. Ian thought the camphor balls were mints. He put one in his mouth, screwed up his face and spat it into his hand while making a dash for the kitchen for something sweet to take the taste away. The girls looked at each other and started laughing and Kathleen thought how pretty they were when they smiled.

The next few weeks proved difficult for the family – especially Joyce: Bill and Kathleen both worked shifts and she'd promised her parents she'd get the children ready for school in the mornings. Bill and Kathleen took turns when it came to preparing the evening meal, depending upon their shifts. In the event that they were both working, Joyce would make the evening meal.

Mornings were to prove the most difficult. The girls were fussy eaters and what one twin liked the other didn't and Karen only ever picked at her food. The boys, on the other hand, were no trouble and ate everything put down to them. Naomi wanted the children to have porridge followed by a boiled egg and toast before they went to school every morning, but she didn't appreciate how long this would take.

The children were frustratingly slow in dressing in the cold, dark mornings and huddled round the paraffin heater in an effort to keep warm. Sometimes Joyce would lose her patience with them then had to remind herself that the children were homesick and missing their mother. When she thought how she would feel if it were her and Ian, it motivated her to fulfil the promise she had made not only to their mother but also to her own parents.

In India they'd been used to having their clothes and shoes laid out for them in the morning, they woke up to sunshine and breakfast was usually cereal followed by fruit and yogurt. The children refused to eat the porridge and would waste time pushing it around the bowl until it was cold. Joyce could empathise with them since she detested the stuff just as much as they did – even the thought of making it in the morning could make her nauseous.

The morning started at six o'clock to get everyone ready for school. Notwithstanding the early start, it still didn't allow sufficient time to meet the demands of Aunt Naomi regarding their dietary requirements; therefore it was unanimously decided that porridge would no longer be served and breakfast would only consist of eggs and toast. There was a resounding cheer at the table and happy faces all round.

One hurdle had been subjugated but another lay ahead and this one was slightly more complicated – the timing of the eggs. John, Shane and Teresa liked theirs medium, while Karen liked hers hard-boiled, and Cecelia preferred hers soft. What could be easier?

It took a bit of ingenuity getting to grips with the procedure and in the beginning everyone was getting the wrong eggs which resulted in absolute chaos. The recently invented felt-tipped pen held the solution. Joyce marked each egg with a corresponding initial, then it was simply a matter of timing – the one marked with the letter 'C' – the soft-boiled egg – came out first, the three medium ones – marked appropriately – came out next and the hard-boiled one marked 'K' came out last at one-minute intervals. Voila!

Thankfully, children can be fickle where eating habits are concerned and boiled eggs every morning soon became repetitive and boring. Consequently, a vote was taken and once again it was unanimously decided that cereal followed by toast and jam was the order of the day. As a rule, most routines eventually become straightforward. This, indisputably, was the case as far as breakfast was concerned and soon Joyce's obligations became fewer as the children gradually became more independent. The only requirement now was to ensure they got to school on time, which they did with the help of Annette.

Joyce was working in the Cartland Bridge Hotel as a waitress after school and at the weekends and at the same time trying to find some quiet study time for her prelims for 'A' levels.

Annette was a great help with the children and as the weeks passed it was evident that some kind of normality had been restored into the daily routine. Joyce established a rota ensuring that each child took their turn with the washing up and cleaning and although it seemed to work initially it rapidly became the source of much animosity amongst the children. Some of them were rubbing out their names and moving their names against those duties which required less effort. Eventually, the rota system was abolished and they were assigned their duties on a daily basis. Normal service was resumed!

Towards the end of March Naomi phoned to say they'd found a house big enough for the family in a location close to work and with excellent schools. The entry date was the middle of May. Despite the fact there had been some pretty stressful times for all the children when Naomi's five first came from India, they had all grown very fond of each other and when they left the house seemed empty without them.

CHAPTER 34

1977

Kathleen hadn't seen her mother for over twenty-five years. The children were married and had children of their own and, like most young families, worked on a budget. Even with the contributions from her children it was only possible to buy one return fare to Australia.

Birdi was getting on in years and Kathleen knew if she didn't go to Australia now she may not get to see her mother before she died. She felt a strong desire to see her mother again and spend time with her before it was too late.

It was the first time Kathleen and Bill had been separated from each other since Kathleen's six-month secondment in Lesmahagow and Bill was going to miss her. He put on a brave face, telling her that she must go and see her mother.

She left on 4th January, two days after their wedding anniversary.

James picked her up at the airport and took her to his house. Birdi and Marie were sitting by the pool and although Kathleen had gone over the reunion in her mind so many times, no words would come. They embraced each other tightly for what seemed like an eternity, with tears of joy running down their cheeks. They stood back and looked at each other, and the realisation of the years they had missed suddenly hit them. There was so much to say yet so little time.

Marie had arranged for Malcolm and Naomi and their families to come over that evening and had been preparing food all day. Norman, Naomi and her three daughters had emigrated to Australia in 1973 but her two sons, John and Shane, decided to stay in England.

The families had arranged for Kathleen to see some of the sights of Perth and surrounding areas, so the next day three cars set off to Yanchep National Park. A lunchtime boat trip had been arranged on Loch McNess and the girls had packed picnic baskets for this. All types of burgers, buns and salads had also been packed for the obligatory Aussie barbeque for the evening which would be cooked by the men on one of the many barbecue areas located in the park.

Family outing at Yanchep National Park
(Birdi second from the left and Kathleen in the middle)

Marie, Kathleen and Naomi at Lake Monger

Kathleen spent many hours with her mother, sitting by the pool, reminiscing about Eden Estate and the good times. She could see that her mother's health wasn't good and was glad she had the chance to see her mother one last time. She wouldn't go back to Australia without Bill and by the time they had saved for the fares her mother would no longer be alive. She had to make each day count.

The five weeks she spent in Australia were the longest five weeks of Bill's life. He wrote to Kathleen every week, keeping her informed of what was happening at home and although he tried to keep his letters upbeat it was clear he was missing her dreadfully.

The day came when Kathleen had to return to Scotland and although she was looking forward to seeing Bill and her family again this was tainted by the thought of saying goodbye, probably for the last time, to her mother. She had requested that nobody came to the airport to see her off and that she'd rather say her goodbyes before they left for the airport. She couldn't face saying goodbye twice to her mother.

CHAPTER 35

───────◦⊙⊙◦───────

Kathleen and Bill both had long careers in the medical profession and it was now time for Bill to retire. A retirement party was planned for the following Saturday and about thirty people were invited, mostly family, friends and some of his colleagues.

Bill and Kathleen made the food for the party. He was a fabulous cook. He often took in different types of curries for his colleagues and the surgeons to taste. They used to tell him he was wasting his time as an ODP and that he should open a restaurant. He had fleetingly toyed with the idea of opening something small in Lanark, but then resigned himself to the fact it was too late in life to start such a venture. Occasionally he'd reflect upon the fact that had they been able to bring money out of India he may have been in a position to open a restaurant, but then he'd remind himself that in the early 1950s there were no Indian restaurants in rural Lanark and even if he did open one, would anyone want to eat there?

There was one dish he prepared which was a favourite with everyone but he didn't have a name for. Kathleen called it 'Burma Bill's Special'. She used to tease him about a Burmese woman he met during the war who gave him the recipe. 'Chow', as it came to be known to the family, was one of those recipes which became timeless by succeeding in traversing four generations. Perhaps he should have opened a restaurant – he undeniably had an aptitude for cooking.

The children had grown up and now had children of their own and all the grandchildren were at the party which was in full swing, with everyone enjoying the food and the music. Their best friends Jock and Jessie were there. Jock had kicked off his shoes and was attempting to demonstrate to Jessie how well he could do the Twist. Two of the surgeons had just come off work having worked long shifts and the younger of the two had fallen asleep after he'd eaten. The laughter from the children on seeing Jock doing the Twist woke him up. At first he was bewildered and as he sat up, he said he'd just had an incredible dream and in the dream he was eating a giant potato crisp. Bill reminded him that just before he fell asleep he'd eaten several papodums.

The children couldn't contain their laughter and were eager to remind him of what they looked like and brought him a plate piled high with papodums.

Kathleen scarcely sat down, taking the grandchildren up in turn in an attempt to teach them how to Jive while Bill was going round making sure everyone had enough to eat and drink. The party had gone well and as everyone left they all said how great the food was and how much they'd enjoyed themselves.

It was Bill's final week at work and on Monday evening when he came home Kathleen noticed him wincing when he walked. She asked him what was wrong and he replied he was in agony most of the day but he was fine when he changed into his shoes for theatre.

When he took his shoes off, Kathleen turned them over and started laughing, pointing out he'd been wearing a size 9, which was Jock's shoe size – they both wore the same style black shoes. It soon became apparent to Jock this was the reason he'd been walking out of his shoes all day – he had Bill's size 10s on!

CHAPTER 36

1989

Kathleen was the matron of Monteith House Nursing Home and had just one year to go before she retired. She was looking forward to her retirement and by this time only worked three days a week. On her days off she and Bill looked forward to visiting places of interest and sightseeing – they both appreciated the beauty of Scotland, even in the winter when the hills had snow on them. It reminded her of when she was a girl in boarding school in Mussoorie, Northern India, in the foothills of the Himalayas when they were covered in snow.

The car had clocked up a hefty mileage and Kathleen persuaded Bill to part with his beloved Cortina and get something newer. However, it would have to meet Bill's criteria of a boot big enough to take the essential folding table and chairs, together with the Primus stove and picnic basket.

After a month of searching, a new Datsun Cherry was chosen, which matched Bill's requirements perfectly. It was economical to run, especially on the longer journeys to Oban which they took frequently, and it met with the prerequisite boot space. The Trossachs and St. Mary's Loch were also great favourites of theirs. On one of their daytrips they had discovered a spot at St. Mary's Loch right on the banks of the loch which was relatively quiet and where Bill could set up his outdoor kitchen. Kathleen used to joke with him saying he'd spent too much time with the natives with all this outdoor cooking and once suggested they should go in somewhere to eat, but Bill preferred to eat al fresco – perhaps she was right about his time with the natives! As they ate, looking out over the loch, they'd reflect upon the beauty of the country that had become their home.

They were discussing where they might go next summer when Kathleen retired and she suggested somewhere in the north of Scotland, but surprisingly Bill asked if she would like to go back to Australia. At first she wondered if he was just saying that to please her but he said he would like to see the family again. Bill had convinced her that he wasn't just doing it for her but that he'd like to see Australia too. So they made plans to go to Australia in 1990 after Kathleen had retired. Birdi had passed away in 1988 but Kathleen's brothers and her sister Naomi were still out there.

1989 – Bill and Kathleen at North Berwick

CHAPTER 37

———❦———

The five-apartment in Melvinhall Road had grown too big for the two of them now the children had all left home and they moved to a smaller house on the other side of the town.

One night Kathleen came home after a particularly busy backshift and felt more tired than usual, so she kissed Bill goodnight and went to bed early. During the night she got up to go to the bathroom but didn't put the light on in case it disturbed Bill.

He never found out if she'd taken a dizzy turn that night or if she had become disorientated in the dark and thought she was in the old house. She fell downstairs and hit her head on the radiator at the bottom of the stairs. Bill heard the noise, put the light on and saw her lying at the bottom of the stairs. He ran downstairs to help her and when he lifted her head he could feel her warm blood on his fingers. He phoned for an ambulance and Kathleen was taken to hospital, suffering from severe head injuries.

CHAPTER 38

⟡

I lost my faith and fell out with God the day he took my mother and hoped she would forgive me for that. How could He forget all the good she had done in caring for others and how ironic was it that she would spend the final years of her life in the care home where she was once the Matron?

After the accident she was in a coma for twelve days and I prayed every day that when she came out of the coma there would be no brain damage, but my worst fears were confirmed. On the twelfth day, when she woke up, it was obvious she'd never be the same again. She'd suffered severe brain trauma from the fall and her speech centre had been damaged irrevocably so anything she said was jumbled and unintelligible.

Two weeks later she was transferred from hospital to Monteith House Nursing Home. As I was clearing out her locker at the hospital prior to her transfer to Monteith House, I came across the notepad I used when trying to teach her to write again and was greatly saddened by the childlike scribbles on the pages. I was flicking through the pages towards the back of the notepad when I came across a couple of lines in her handwriting, where she wrote: *'It must be Spring because I can see the daffodils from my window.'*

I quickly flicked through the pages to see if there was anything else to give my father hope, but every page was blank. Then I picked up the envelope containing those little samples for choosing paint colours which I used to try and get her to recognise the colours and cried when I thought back to how irritated she became when she would throw the crayons on the floor when she couldn't remember. On reflection, I think it was her way of telling us that she didn't want to live without quality of life and wanted nothing else but to be left alone. I still feel remorse when I think of those visits and the precious time wasted trying to motivate her, which ultimately achieved nothing except to make her unhappy when I should have been treasuring every moment with her.

I think she was aware of her limitations at that point, although I still prayed and believed He'd intervene and that somehow she might recover. I always hoped she would respond, but deep down I knew she'd given up and reconciled herself to the cruel twist of fate that awaited her.

My father never missed a day visiting his beautiful Katy. I used to go with him on the weekends to visit her and we'd make sure the gas curling tongs and her make-up were packed. The first thing I'd do was to get her hair done and put on her make-up. She always wore a beautiful shade of coral lipstick which complimented the colour of her skin. My dad loved to see his Katy come back to life, even for just an hour or two. I got the feeling she still knew who he was because after her make-over she'd look up at him with her lovely almond-shaped eyes and the slightest hint of a smile would play on her lips. At least I like to think so.

She knew her life was over and had given up. She often said to me that if she had the misfortune to end up like her patients she hoped I would help her to die. It must have been a long four years for her, trapped inside a body which no longer fully functioned yet still being partially aware of where she was. He couldn't have been more cruel to someone who had devoted her life to caring for others, or could He?

Her inheritance eventually came through when she was in the care home. The proceeds from the sale of Eden Estate had never been invested in the forty or so years the money had been frozen, which resulted in each sibling receiving only £9,000. The money was no use to her now and my father used some of it to buy her a new state-of-the-art reclining chair to support her frail body – he always felt she looked uncomfortable propped up for hours in the relatively hard chair the home provided. Fortunately for her, she only occupied it for a couple of months. She died on 3rd September 1994 and my father died a few months later on 7th April 1995 from a heart attack – or maybe it was a broken heart.

I'm glad she found her true vocation. I've always believed one's life is planned from the start. She'd originally set out to be a teacher but fate dealt the hand which put her on a different path. She hoped she would get a teaching post in the school in Lanark, but had she done so, the nursing profession would have lost a great nurse and a compassionate, caring person who was totally committed to her patients.

People still remember her to this day and often tell me how kind she was when they were ill – one woman, who looked to be about forty, told me that my mother delivered her! I had difficulty suppressing my laughter.

Each of the people's lives she touched will have their own reasons for remembering her, but I will always remember her as a beautiful person both inside and out – my mentor, my friend, my Mother.

Kathleen and Bill (behind) on their first ever holiday abroad,
arriving in Majorca in January 1973.

Mum and Dad

Lightning Source UK Ltd.
Milton Keynes UK
UKHW02f0614181217
314677UK00008B/296/P